ABOUT ISLAND PRESS

Island Press, a nonprofit organization, publishes, markets, and distributes the most advanced thinking on the conservation of our natural resources—books about soil, land, water, forests, wildlife, and hazardous and toxic wastes. These books are practical tools used by public officials, business and industry leaders, natural resource managers, and concerned citizens working to solve both local and global resource problems.

Founded in 1978, Island Press reorganized in 1984 to meet the increasing demand for substantive books on all resource-related issues. Island Press publishes and distributes under its own imprint and offers these services to other nonprofit organizations.

Support for Island Press is provided by Apple Computer, Inc., Mary Reynolds Babcock Foundation, Geraldine R. Dodge Foundation, The Energy Foundation, The Charles Engelhard Foundation, The Ford Foundation, Glen Eagles Foundation, The George Gund Foundation, William and Flora Hewlett Foundation, The Joyce Foundation, The John D. and Catherine T. MacArthur Foundation, The Andrew W. Mellon Foundation, The Joyce Mertz-Gilmore Foundation, The New-Land Foundation, The J. N. Pew, Jr. Charitable Trust, Alida Rockefeller, The Rockefeller Brothers Fund, The Florence and John Schumann Foundation, The Tides Foundation, and individual donors.

NATURE TOURISM

NATURE TOURISM

Managing for the Environment

EDITED BY TENSIE WHELAN

Foreword by Peter A. A. Berle,
President
National Audubon Society

ISLAND PRESS

Washington, D.C. • *Covelo, California*

Library of Congress Cataloging-in-Publication Data

Nature tourism : managing for the environment / edited by Tensie Whelan : foreword by Peter A. A. Berle.
    p. cm.
  Includes bibliographical references and index.
  ISBN 1-55963-037-X (cloth).—ISBN 1-55963-036-1 (paper)
  1. Tourist trade—Environmental aspects. I. Whelan, Tensie.
G155.A1N39 1991
338.4'791—dc   91-2646
                                           CIP

Printed on recycled, acid-free paper

Manufactured in the United States of America

10 9 8 7 6 5 4 3 2 1

*This book is dedicated to Johan Åshuvud,
whose vision sustained me throughout its
production, and Eric Wright, whose willingness to help made it possible for me to complete the book only two months after my
deadline. I also dedicate the book to my
daughter Lora-Faye, and hope that in twenty
years she will still be able to visit the unique
and wonderful places ecotourists visit today.*
—TW

CONTENTS

Foreword

My family and I have long been outdoor enthusiasts. We backpack, cross-country ski, canoe, fish, and climb mountains large and small. We have never thought of ourselves as "ecotourists," but in retrospect, we are. We have traveled to some magnificent natural areas. Hopefully some of the dollars spent in the process have contributed to preserve these places, either directly, or through supporting local communities. As competition for open spaces and natural resources intensifies, ecotourism can provide the economic rationale for preserving rather than destroying nature's bounty.

This book, *Nature Tourism: Managing for the Environment*, takes a tough and much-needed look at ecotourism—its promise and its pitfalls. Editor Tensie Whelan has brought together experts from around the world to make thoughtful and well-researched contributions to the debate. Part One, on ecotourism destinations, provides a clear and fascinating introduction to the pros and cons of the industry. The reader learns about government planning gone awry, ill-educated tourists destroying the very resource they have come to visit, and the fury of local inhabitants who have not benefited from the tourist visits. But we also learn about the quiet beauty of a sunny Costa Rican destination, the major contribution ecotourism has made to Kenya's economy, and the new hope for ranchers struggling to survive in the Rocky Mountain states.

Part Two, a framework for developing environmentally beneficial ecotourism, will be extremely helpful for students of the phenomenon, environmental organizations, the ecotourism industry, host governments, and local citizens. It provides understandable guidelines on how to undertake a cost-benefit analysis of a potential tourism site; invaluable insight into how to market an ecotourism destination; and useful suggestions on how to ensure local participation in a project, among other fine chapters.

And for the reader who wants to take this in at a glance, Tensie Whelan's overview provides a unique and carefully researched introduction to ecotourism—what it is, what it could be, and how to improve it.

The National Audubon Society was one of the first providers of ecotourism travel in the United States. As early as 1940, we were running trips in Florida, Texas, and Virginia. Today, our tours to the tropics, the North and South Pole, and unique ecosystems in the United States attract thousands of Audubon members and other ecotourists. Participation in these trips provides travelers with a renewed respect and appreciation for nature. I have often seen Audubon ecotourists come home and ask what they can do to help the places they have visited. "How can I ensure that habitat and its wildlife will be here for my children and the children of others across the world?" they ask.

At Audubon, ecotourism is part of a way of life. Our ecotourism principles, outlined in Chapter 1, ensure that both our outfitters and our tourists develop the potential of ecotourism, while avoiding its pitfalls. Other organizations have begun to do the same. I hope that this book, and others like it, will help make environmentally sensitive ecotourism a way of life for us all, sooner rather than later. We haven't much time.

Peter A. A. Berle, President
National Audubon Society

PART I

A Visit to Key Destinations

CHAPTER 1

Ecotourism and Its Role in Sustainable Development

Tensie Whelan

I became fascinated with the potential of ecotourism while working as a journalist in Central America. I was in the region to write about sustainable development and its role in the conservation of the region's unique and beautiful natural resources. Over and over again, I saw small chunks of the environment being saved by people who had an economic interest in doing so, whether it was villagers saving rain forest habitat in order to raise iguanas for sale, or private individuals preserving and maintaining virgin rain forest as an attraction for tourists.

There are intense economic pressures on the people of Central America and elsewhere, including the developed world, to overexploit their natural resources. Many countries have established protected areas to guard against this. However, when the only way to obtain a meal is to mine the resources of a protected area, the protected area is going to lose. If we are to save any of our precious environment, we must provide people with alternatives to destruction.

3

Ecotourism, done well, can be a sustainable and relatively simple alternative. It promises employment and income to local communities and needed foreign exchange to national governments, while allowing the continued existence of the natural resource base. In fact, it cannot survive unless the resource on which it is based is protected. It can empower local communities, giving them a sense of pride in their natural resources and control over their communities' development. It can educate travelers about the importance of the ecosystems they visit and actively involve them in conservation efforts. In sum, it has the potential to maximize economic benefits and minimize environmental costs.

Its potential is not always realized, however, and it can destroy both the environment and local communities. My goal in this book is to assess ecotourism's role in the sustainable development of natural areas and to answer the question: How can ecotourism be planned so that it is both ecologically sensitive and economically productive? Toward that end, I have divided this book into two parts: the first examines several case studies to see what has worked and what hasn't; the second section provides more technical information on how to do ecotourism "right."

TOURISM IS BIG BUSINESS

According to the World Tourism Organization (WTO, a UN affiliate), tourism is the second largest industry in the world, comprising 7 percent of the world trade in goods and services, and producing $195 billion annually in domestic and international receipts. That was 390 million international tourists in 1988 (up 20 million from 1987), creating 74 million jobs in tourism (up from 65 million). In developing countries, tourism comprises one-third of their trade in goods and services. WTO projects that tourism will become the world's largest industry by the year 2000 (WTO 1989). WTO also found that adventure travel (which includes ecotourism in the WTO definition) enjoyed almost 10 percent of the market in 1989 and is increasing at the rate of 30 percent a year (Kallen 1990).

In the United States, the U.S. Department of Commerce estimates that by the year 2000, international tourism revenues will reach $30 billion (Edgell 1987). While no formal studies have been done, tour operators say that ecotourism makes up a significant portion of the total.

Conversely, the editor of the U.S.-based *Speciality Travel Index* estimates that special-interest travel by U.S. citizens to sites outside the United States comprises 3 to 5 percent of the total, and that ecotourism is responsible for up to half of that figure.

The developing world currently is the recipient of some $55 billion in tourism receipts (Westlake 1989), and a good portion of those expenditures is related to ecotourism. Kenya earns $350 million in tourism receipts annually, for example, almost entirely due to wildlife tourism. In Costa Rica, where 60 percent of visitors are interested in visiting the national parks system (Boo 1990), tourism-related foreign exchange came to $138 million in 1986, and all the signs point to a sizable increase since then. Ecuador, and more specifically the Galápagos Islands, brought $180 million in foreign exchange in 1986, again mostly for ecotourism (Healy 1988).

WHO IS THE INTREPID ECOTOURIST?

Most ecotourists are from Europe, North America, and Japan, as they have more money and more leisure time than many of their counterparts in developing countries. The average U.S. ecotourist is a man or woman familiar with the outdoors, a professional or retired, between thirty-one and fifty years of age, who most likely has had previous experience traveling abroad. One-third of all ecotourists are reported by tour operators to be repeat customers (Ingram and Durst 1987)!

These ecotourists are relatively wealthy; a survey of U.S. travelers to Ecuador found that approximately 25 percent of

Figure 1.1   *Sariska Tiger Reserve near Jaipur, India.*

the group earned over $90,000 a year in family income, and that another 27 percent earned between $30,000 and $60,000 (Wilson 1987). Another study showed that ecotourists are likely to spend more money than other tourists, at least in Latin America, where people who cited national parks as their main reason for entering the country spent over $1,000 more in two weeks than did other tourists (Boo 1990).

The most popular activities for ecotourists are trekking/ hiking, bird watching, nature photography, wildlife safaris, camping, mountain climbing, fishing, river rafting/canoe-ing/kayaking, and botanical study. Nepal, Kenya, Tanzania, China, Mexico, Costa Rica, and Puerto Rico are the most popular destinations (Ingram and Durst 1987).

Ecotourism is popular also in the United States; in 1989, there were 265 million recreational visits (both domestic and international) to the national parks system alone (deCourcy Hinds 1990). Wyoming estimates total expenditures related to the consumptive and nonconsumptive use of its unique wildlife resource at nearly $1 billion annually (Kruckenberg 1988).

Why has ecotourism become so popular? No comprehensive studies have been undertaken, but speculation is rife. Many ecotourists come from urban or suburban settings; they may feel the need to "get back in touch with nature." Others may feel bored with their nine-to-five routine, and wish for the challenge and excitement to be found in an untamed environment. The popular media bring sights and sounds of exotic locales into everyone's living rooms, subtly promoting natural areas, while the recent publicity surrounding the loss of ecotourism sites due to deforestation and other factors may provide people with an incentive to see them before it's too late. Others may travel because they have already developed an interest in birding or river rafting in their own countries, and wish to see how it's done elsewhere.

ECOTOURISM: WHAT WORKS, WHAT DOESN'T

It is clear that ecotourism has the financial potential to provide a viable economic alternative to the exploitation of the environment. The following is one example of an ecotourism project that has lived up to its promise.

In Costa Rica, a unique, locally based ecotourism project called "Rara Avis" has been highly successful in saving threatened rain forest, making money, getting the locals involved, and educating visitors.

Rara Avis is a private reserve perched high in the mountains and bordering the national park, Braulio Carrillo. Visitors are brought by jeep from the capital of San José to the closest village to the site, Horquetas. They are driven by villagers to a small local "soda," where they stop and have lunch. They park in the dirt yard of the program manager.

Over lunch, they discover that he is a former Costa Rican forest service employee who now believes that it is important to keep the rain forest standing. Several locals stop by and chat with the tourists while they are waiting for the jeeps to be loaded with supplies—virtually all the food for the trip is bought in the village of Horquetas. Once the jeeps are loaded, they make their way up the mountain until they come to a crude but comfortable bunkhouse (formerly a prison barracks!), where local Costa Ricans welcome them with a home-cooked dinner by lamplight.

Rara Avis has involved the local community in every aspect of its tours. In fact, ecotourism has now become the third most important source of income for the inhabitants of Horquetas. Not surprisingly, all are favorably disposed toward the project.

In the case of Rara Avis, ecotourism was used as a technique to help save the rain forest right from the beginning. However, in some cases, ecotourism can be developed after a protected area has been created, if problems with local communities require that economic alternatives to the exploitation of the protected areas be created.

In India, "Project Tiger," a governmental plan to save the tiger by creating national parks around its habitat, is threatened by the lack of local support. Here, planners neglected to involve the members of the community, to provide them with incentives for conservation, or even to suggest alternatives for fuelwood and grazing grounds. Consequently, some 55,000 cattle currently reside within the buffer zone of Ranthambhor National Park, one of the key protected areas in the plan, often wandering into the core area, and competing for fodder with the tiger's natural prey. People continue to gather fuelwood from the forest.

The Antaeus Group, a nonprofit educational and research institute, sees ecotourism as a way out of this problem. It plans to bring tourists into the Ranthambhor and involve them in local conservation efforts. The accommodations and food for these travelers will be generated locally, and the Antaeus Group will also make direct donations to community development projects with each expedition.

This is the role ecotourism could play, but more often it fails to attain its potential.

PROBLEMS OF LOCAL PARTICIPATION

One of the most egregious shortcomings of most ecotourism projects is that the local people are not given any role in the planning process or implementation and are forced off lands that were traditionally theirs to use. Not surprisingly, they become resentful of the "rich tourists" who supplant them, but, more important, economic needs make it difficult for them not to overexploit the resources of the protected area. Firewood, meat, agricultural land, sale of exotic wildlife—these means of subsistence have been removed, often with no viable alternative. And a high population rate means that they have an increasing number of mouths to feed.

In Costa Rica, the planning associated with the country's spectacular parks system took place on a national, not a local, level. People were moved off their lands and told they would be compensated for the loss. Many have not yet been paid. Occasionally, they were discouraged from entering the parks at all, and in many cases, important sources of income were suddenly no longer available. Not surprisingly, many Costa Ricans living near the national parks are often responsible for slash-and-burn, gold mining, and a host of other activities within park boundaries. In recent years, government agencies and conservation organizations have begun to turn toward a more localized approach, with an emphasis on sustainable development as a solution.

Another problem is that income generated by tourism is very likely to almost completely bypass the local communities. In Nepal, for example, where local communities provide shelter and hospitality to trekkers, only $0.20 of the $3 spent daily by the trekker stays in the villages (Puntenney 1990).

Foreign tour operators are a large part of the problem in most countries. Very often, they bring in their own supplies and staff and hire few natives to assist on their trips. A survey of thirty-two U.S.-based operators (41 percent of all U.S. ecotour operators) found that while twenty used local guides and interpreters, only eight employed local managers or tour operators, six used local cooks, and eight used local drivers (Ingram and Durst 1987). And though twenty report they use local guides, it is likely that most are brought in from the larger cities and are not from the small communities where the tour takes place. The same survey found that while 40 percent of U.S. ecotour operators use rural and village accommodations, 21 percent use luxury hotels, 33 percent use other hotels, and 27 percent camp out (operators use more than one type of accommodation).

The national economy of the host country is likely to do substantially better than the local economy; one study found that at least 50 percent of tourist expenditures in developing countries are likely to stay in the country (English 1986). However, it is unusual to find those receipts (e.g., tourism taxes) channeled back to local communities or even to the management of the protected areas that generated the income.

FUNDS FOR PROTECTED AREA MANAGEMENT

There are roughly 1,000 national parks in the world today, mostly in the developed countries. Fewer than half of the developing countries contain national parks. While most countries do have some protected areas—there are 7,000 protected areas around the globe—the protection is often only on paper, due to both a lack of funds and local support. Yet the success of ecotourism is dependent on the continued existence of these protected areas.

Over and over again, we find parks in crisis because very few funds are being dedicated to their management and protection. Often countries focus their attention on purchasing lands, but then fail to follow up with adequate funds for infrastructure and management. This is true in Costa Rica, where spending for parks (excluding acquisition) has remained at the same level for ten years; in Kenya, where until recently only $7 million of the $300 million generated by parks was returned to them; and in the United States, where park rangers have to supplement their salaries with food stamps, and parks such as the Adirondack National Park have become battlegrounds for developers. These economic problems are sometimes compounded by the fact that parks in developing countries charge woefully inadequate entry fees to foreign visitors, who can afford to pay a great deal more than the locals.

Private reserves also have emphasized acquisition at the expense of management. The privately owned Monteverde Cloud Forest Reserve in Costa Rica, for example, has mounted a highly successful campaign to raise funds for land acquisition. However, while the land can support the number of current visitors, the current infrastructure can not. In response, the reserve is currently conducting a feasibility study on developing a visitor's center and new trails.

CARRYING CAPACITIES

Ironically, the survival of protected areas may be threatened by the very thing that otherwise protects them—tourism. All protected areas have limited ecological and aesthetic carrying capacities. The ecological carrying capacity is reached when the number of visitors and characteristics of visitor use start to affect the wildlife and degrade the ecosystem (e.g., disrupting mating habits and eroding soil). The aesthetic carrying capacity is reached when tourists encounter so many other tourists, or see the impacts of other visitors (e.g., lack of watchable wildlife, litter, erosion, deforestation), that their enjoyment of the site is marred.

A survey of visitors to the Spanish Peaks Primitive Area in the United States, for example, found that if the number of trail encounters were to increase from three to four, people would be less willing to pay, but enough would continue to come so that the payoff in terms of increased revenues would more than offset the loss. However, when the number of expected trail encounters increases to five, the willingness to pay becomes so low that the aggregate drops off sharply and the area begins to lose money (Lindberg 1990).

While establishing the ecological capacity for a protected area seems essential, very few areas in the developing and developed worlds alike have identified carrying capacities. Nor have they determined how to avoid exceeding those carrying capacities.

In some areas, such as Antarctica, this is because no one agency or organization is responsible for monitoring or managing the environmental impacts of visitation. The *Bahia Paraiso*, a supply ship carrying tourists to the Antarctic, crashed upon uncharted rocks in 1989, leaking 200,000 gallons of diesel fuel, which killed thousands of seabirds and marine mammals and disrupted migration patterns. The ship was outside charted waters because the tourists had wanted to try a different route. Tourist ships also dump garbage directly into the ocean, and tourists wander into delicate areas, removing "souvenirs" and disrupting ecosystems. This occurs at least in part because there is no one responsible for establishing or enforcing guidelines against environmentally destructive behavior.

The rapid increase in the number of ecotourists has overloaded fragile areas. Nepal has seen the number of its tourists increase fivefold, from 45,000 in 1970 to 223,000 in 1986. Over the same period, the number of ecotourists (trekkers, mostly) almost tripled, from 12,600 to 33,600. This has resulted in the emergence virtually overnight of more than 200 mountain lodges and the clearing of large areas in order to supply fuelwood for lodges and trekkers. The visitor use of fuelwood for cooking, hot showers, and campfires is extravagant—a typical two-month climbing expedition may use as much as 8,000 kg of fuelwood, while a traditional hearth burns 5,000 kg in one year (Puntenney 1990).

In the United States, many of the more accessible national and state parks are overwhelmed during the peak summer months. In Minnesota, where problems resemble those of other states, visits to the state's sixty-four parks increased from 6 million to 10 million in three years. Ten of the parks are subject to continual overcrowding. Increased visitation to parks nationwide has resulted in more roads, more parking lots, and more concessions built in the protected areas, frequently decreasing the aesthetic value of the park.

Often, park managers, conservationists, and governments determine to solve their carrying capacity problems by emphasizing quality rather than quantity. In other words, they target fewer people who can pay more. This may make sense from an environmental point of view, but it has elitist implications. In Rwanda, for example, visitors pay $170 a day to see Dian Fossey's gorillas in their mountain reserve. In order to keep the reserve accessible to Rwandans, the fee charged to locals is minimal. However, the reserve is no longer accessible to many foreign tourists. If this trend means that ecotourism becomes an industry only for the rich, then average citizens will not be able to learn about other environments and wildlife and will be less inclined to fund or support protection efforts.

NATIONAL AND INTERNATIONAL ENVIRONMENTAL PRESSURES

Environmental problems in protected areas are not only caused by tourism or local population pressures. The Adirondack National Park in the United States is suffering from acid rain produced thousands of miles away, for example. Water diversion from the Everglades has severely disrupted that system. The soil released by deforestation of Caribbean isles is carried by rivers into the ocean, where it kills marine life in underwater parks, and the chemical pollution in East European rivers runs through refuges, killing plant and aquatic life.

These issues are outside the scope of this book. Nevertheless, it is important to remember that the impact of ecotourism and even local use of resources may be much less harmful than these other environmental impacts in the long term, and ecotourism planners must take them into account as well.

CONFLICTING MANAGEMENT OBJECTIVES

Protected areas supporting ecotourism often are managed by a number of agencies with conflicting goals and objectives. Nearly thirty agencies manage some aspect of the Greater Yellowstone Ecosystem, for example, which makes it virtually impossible to develop a coherent management or ecotourism policy for the area. In other cases, some agencies have a mandate to exploit the land, as in the Tongass National Forest in Alaska, where the single-minded, and uneconomic, pursuit of timber is causing severe problems for a growing ecotourism industry. In Costa Rica, agencies often have conflicting needs for natural areas, ranging from developing hydroelectricity to logging.

Conflicting goals and needs are not only the province of governmental agencies. Government, conservationists, local communities, tour operators, and development agencies all need to resolve their differences and work together if ecotourism really is to be sustainable. This needs to occur on both a national and an international level.

Governments ought to develop national ecotourism boards composed of representatives from every related industry and concern. These boards would be responsible for weighing different alternatives, based on all pertinent information, rather than focusing on the specific factors that concern a particular party. They would be given a mandate by the government to develop economically and environmentally sustainable ecotourism.

Some of the constraints of ecotourism are due to the fact that it is an international activity. Many tourists are from other countries, as are ecotour operators and major carriers. All would benefit from an international forum for discussion. In addition, many countries do not have the resources they need to manage the development of ecotourism wisely. Access to an international body that provides needed technical and financial assistance, as well as access to information and others experiencing similar concerns, would be invaluable. However, no international organization focusing specifically on ecotourism currently exists.

THE ECOTOURIST AS ACTIVIST

The ecotourist will be a key player in the success or failure of ecotourism. In Monteverde, the nesting of quetzals occasionally is disrupted by tourists who rap on their nests and then stand poised with a video camera to capture their flight. In Yellowstone, visitors feed the bears, encouraging them to accost people for food and making them extremely dangerous. In the Caribbean, tourists buy jewelry made from black coral and other rare reef marine life. In Botswana, tourists treat natives with a rude curiosity, not asking for permission to enter their villages and take photographs. Trekkers in Nepal and elsewhere leave behind the litter from the food and other items they have carried in.

Ecotour operators must instill a conservation ethic for environmentally sensitive travel in their clients if they are to continue bringing visitors to fragile sites. The National Audubon Society, which conducts ecotourism tours in many countries, has developed a travel ethic that must be adhered to by all its tour operators. The basic guidelines are as follows:

1. Wildlife and their habitats must not be disturbed.
2. Audubon tourism to natural areas will be sustainable.
3. Waste disposal must have neither environmental nor aesthetic impacts.
4. The experience a tourist gains in traveling with Audubon must enrich his or her appreciation of nature, conservation, and the environment.
5. Audubon tours must strengthen the conservation effort and enhance the natural integrity of places visited.

6. Traffic in products that threaten wildlife and plant populations must not occur.
7. The sensibilities of other cultures must be respected.

Audubon tour operators are required to sign a contract stating that they agree to abide by these strictures. Audubon passengers receive a copy of the guidelines and are asked by questionnaire at the end of the trip if the tour operator followed the ethic. So far, Audubon has not received negative feedback.

The ecotourist can do more than learn from the experience. He or she can get involved. Some tour operators are running tours to areas that have suffered from overuse; clients help clean up the mess left behind by previous visitors and work to restore endangered habitats. Some organizations such as Earthwatch involve tourists in "citizen scientist" activities: counting turtle eggs on the beaches of Costa Rica, for example. On returning home, quite a few tourists become involved with such issues as tropical deforestation and illegal traffic in endangered species.

Ecotour operators and conservation organizations both in the destination country and in the home country need to work harder to get the ecotourist actively involved in sustainable development. Ecotourists represent a potential army of recruits with free time and money to spend on sustainable development efforts.

THE ECOTOURISM DEBATE: WHERE DO WE GO FROM HERE?

The types of issues covered in this chapter are just beginning to be discussed seriously by academics, development assistance agencies, conservation organizations, and government planners. This book differs from previous studies in that it analyzes each of the major components that make ecotourism successful or unsuccessful and provides guidelines on how to make ecotourism work. The first part of the book, "A

Visit to Key Destinations," provides a description and analysis of the ecotourism destinations—Kenya, Costa Rica, and the Greater Yellowstone Ecosystem in the United States. Here we see what has worked and what hasn't, as described by experts in each country.

The second part, "The Nuts and Bolts of Successful Nature Tourism," is more technical in nature; it covers each of the major components of ecotourism—planning an ecotourism development strategy, performing an economic analysis of the alternatives, developing local participation, preparing a marketing strategy—and presents new ideas about how ecotourism can be supported internationally.

Following are brief summaries of each of the chapters.

The former director of the Kenya Wildlife Department, Perez Olindo, takes us through the history of ecotourism in Kenya—how hunting, which had been the first form of tourism in Kenya, was banned in 1978, due to the severe decline of Kenyan wildlife. The tourism infrastructure that had developed to service the hunters was without any tourists. Ingeniously, Kenyans reached out to a new audience—ecotourists—who would come to Kenya to shoot with their cameras. Within a few years, ecotourism was a booming business, in part due to a major marketing effort on the part of the government. However, problems emerged. The mismanagement of the relationship of ecotourism to the locals precipitated unnecessary conflict. A lack of funding for parks management, as well as inadequate information about carrying capacities, is threatening the long-term viability of the parks. Fortunately, the Kenyan government has taken steps to improve the management of the parks and is trying to get the locals involved. International cooperation on ivory has led to a marked decline in the number of elephants slaughtered illegally, while direct payments to local communities have also decreased local poaching.

Yanina Rovinski, a Costa Rican writer specializing in environment and development issues and a consultant on ecotourism, documents how science-based tourism—in which scientists came to Costa Rica to study tropical biology, botany, and wildlife—developed into more broad-based ecotourism. Both are rooted in Costa Rica's extensive system of protected areas. In the early days of the parks, locals were not included in planning, nor were they allowed to use the natural resources of the parks. However, in recent years, the emphasis has shifted to stress more local involvement, with particular emphasis on ecotourism. Ecotourism is nevertheless hampered by the fact that the National Parks Service lacks funds for building infrastructure and management. And the government tourism authority refuses to put money into promoting Costa Rica as a ecotourism destination, preferring instead to focus on beach tourism and large-scale resort schemes.

In the United States, the oldest park in the world, Yellowstone, is under attack by neighboring development schemes and poorly managed ecotourism. Dennis Glick, a wildland planner and analyst with the Greater Yellowstone Coalition, describes the history of the Greater Yellowstone Ecosystem and the problems it currently faces. He shows that ecotourism is making a strong contribution to the economies of the host states and local communities. However, it is being developed helter-skelter, without the benefit of a master plan, often resulting in negative social and environmental impacts.

Bill Bryan describes an exciting new form of ecotourism that is developing in the Yellowstone area—ranch and farm hospitality operations. Working family farms and ranches, facing severe economic problems, have begun to supplement their income with tourist dollars. They offer accommodations and the opportunity to experience the "great outdoors" to urban dwellers. In the states of Wyoming, Montana, and Idaho, these types of endeavors are popping up every day—in 1985, there were five in operation; today there are more than seventy.

Paul Sherman and John Dixon, both environmental economists, explain how to analyze a potential ecotourism project from two angles: financial and social. Ecotourism needs to be looked at as a business and as a type of resource use that helps ensure other, long-term social goals. The net financial and social benefits of ecotourism must be better than the next best alternative if the land under dispute is to be used to its best capacity. Sherman and Dixon then explain how to undertake a cost-benefit analysis for this particular type of project, as well as how to maximize both financial and social benefits. They present several case studies that show how the process works in real life.

Susan Drake, United Nations officer (and formerly local wetlands coordinator) at the U.S. Environmental Protection Agency, defines different levels of local participation and reviews various approaches in the United States and abroad. Her nine-phase local participation plan is based on lessons learned from these other approaches and requires extensive consultation with local communities during planning, implementation, and follow-up in order to address their needs and concerns.

Richard Ryel, president of the largest American ecotour organization, International Expeditions, and his colleague, Tom Grasse, discuss what they have learned about marketing ecotourism during ten years in the business. First, they say, a tour operator must develop a conservation ethic on which the organization should base its activities. Other steps include determining a site's marketability, defining the market, identifying marketing vehicles, crafting the message, getting it out, and developing a mailing list. They emphasize that the ecotourism operator must always consider issues broader than pure monetary concerns, though, of course, making a profit is essential.

Liz Boo, ecotourism program officer at World Wildlife Fund-U.S., puts the problems associated with ecotourism into perspective with her recommendations on how to plan a nature tourism development strategy. She stresses the need for a national ecotourism board, which will help oversee and coordinate the planning of the various government agencies, park managers, tour operators, local conservation organizations, and international conservation and development organizations. She provides specific recommendations for action by each of these sectors in three phases: planning, development, and management. The emphasis is on maximizing the economic benefits of ecotourism, while minimizing negative environmental and social impacts.

Megan Wood, president of Ecoventures (an environmental communications company), contends that ecotourism will need an international forum if it is to succeed. She suggests the creation of an Ecotourism Society, to be composed of specialists in many different fields: tour operators and guides, government representatives, protected area managers, representatives from local communities, conservationists, and development agencies. The society would offer its members the opportunity to develop a global initiative for the sustainable development of ecotourism areas. It would focus on issues such as obtaining technical and financial assistance from the development community, developing environmental principles and guidelines, ensuring local participation, and providing a clearinghouse for information on ecotourism.

CONCLUSION

Ecotourism will not on its own save disappearing ecosystems. Nor will it alone liberate rural communities from the shackles of poverty. In fact, unless it is planned to minimize environmental damage, maximize economic outcomes, and involve the local communities, then it may actually harm the environment and local peoples.

But when ecotourism is planned as a tool for sustainable development, one that includes the type of safeguards discussed in this book, it can indeed make an important contribution to the welfare of both the visited and the visitors and every aspect of the environment. The challenge is to make sure that ecotourism doesn't occur willy-nilly wherever there is a demand for it, but that governments, tour operators, conservation groups, and local communities, among others, plan together where ecotourism sites should be established and how they should be managed. Then, fifty years from now, it will be possible for our grandchildren to enjoy the natural beauty and benefits associated with natural areas near their homes and farther afield.

REFERENCES

Boo, Elizabeth. 1990. *Ecotourism: The Potentials and Pitfalls.* Washington, D.C.: World Wildlife Fund-U.S.

deCourcy Hinds, M. 1990. "Anxious Armies of Vacationers Are Demanding More from Nature." *New York Times* (July 8).

Edgell, D. 1987. *International Tourism Prospects 1987–2000.* Washington, D.C.: U.S. Dept. of Commerce.

English, P. 1986. *The Great Escape? An Examination of North-South Tourism.* Ottawa, Canada: The North-South Institute.

Healy, R. G. 1988. *Economic Consideration in Nature-Oriented Tourism: The Case of Tropical Forest Tourism.* FPEI Working Paper, no. 39. Research Triangle Park, North Carolina: Forest Private Enterprise Initiative.

Ingram, C. D. and P. B. Durst. 1987. *Nature-Oriented Travel to Developing Countries.* FPEI Working Paper, no. 28. Research Triangle Park, North Carolina: Forestry Private Enterprise Initiative.

Kallen, C. 1990. "Ecotourism: The Light at the End of the Terminal." *E Magazine* (July/August).

Kruckenberg, L. 1988. "Wyoming's Wildlife—Worth the Watching: Management in Transition." In *Transactions of the Fifty-third North American Wildlife and Natural Resources Conference.* Reprint.

Lindberg, K. 1990. "Tourism as a Conservation Tool." Working paper. Washington, D.C.: World Resources Institute.

Puntenney, P. J. 1990. "Defining Solutions: The Annapurna Experience." *Cultural Survival Monthly* 14, no. 2.

Westlake, M. 1989. "Riding the Tourist Boom." *South* (August).

Wilson, M. 1987. *Nature-Oriented Tourism in Ecuador: Assess-

ment of Industry Structure and Development Needs. Forestry Private Enterprise Initiative Working Paper No. 20. Raleigh, N.C.: North Carolina State University.

World Tourism Organization (WTO). 1989. *Policy and Activities for Tourism and the Environment.* Madrid: WTO.

CHAPTER 2

The Old Man of Nature Tourism: Kenya

PEREZ OLINDO

In the flatlands of Kenya's Amboseli Game Reserve, a lioness lies resting. Every few minutes, a minivan or bus drives up and the crowd of tourists inside snap their camera shutters. The animal may remain for two hours. In that time, twenty-five vehicles might stop and stare.

Kenya is the world's foremost ecotourist attraction. Some 650 thousand people visit Kenya's parks and protected areas each year, spending about $350 million. Wildlife is the magnet. One estimate holds that an elephant is worth about $14,375 a year, or $900,000 over the course of its life, in tourist expenditures.

This financial success hides a multitude of problems, however. Kenya's colonial legacy, combined with a low level of local community support for the parks, inadequate funding and enforcement powers for the ministry in charge of the parks, and poaching for ivory, has led to a dramatic decline in the elephant population, as well as the degradation of public lands. In response, the Kenyan government has

launched recently a series of innovative techniques and programs it hopes will ensure ecotourism's continued success.

HISTORY OF ECOTOURISM IN KENYA

At the turn of the twentieth century, Kenya was teeming
with a wide array of wildlife. The various ethnic groups of
African peoples moved freely across the land, fishing, hunting, or gathering roots and fruits for a living. They killed
game only as needed for food and rituals, and never for pleasure.

Then the European explorers disembarked on the shores
of the African continent. With their arrival, the first wild animals were captured and killed for sport and other nonessen-
tial uses. In the late nineteenth century, the "great white
hunters" descended on Africa. They made fortunes by selling
ivory, killing hundreds of thousands of elephants. By World
War I, elephant herds in Kenya and the rest of East Africa
were beginning to show serious signs of decline.

Following the war, environmental degradation in the region began, through bush clearing, tilling the land, and
shooting wild animals. The colonial powers, having carved
Africa into areas of influence, encouraged their citizens to
settle there, and tried to turn the "empty" continent into an
agricultural giant.

The attempt was initially unsuccessful due to a basic ig-
norance on the part of the settlers of tropical conditions and
constraints. Imported dairy and beef cattle died by the thousands, unable to adapt to tropical heat and diseases. Crops
were decimated by the forays of African wildlife.

In response, the colonial governments embarked on a
scheme that called for the large-scale elimination of African
wildlife as a means of opening up the country to development. European soldiers who had elected to remain in Africa
after the war were deployed as game wardens.

These game wardens licensed and supervised the activities of the white hunting fraternity. They also hunted themselves. But at the same time, they prevented the African

people from hunting on the pretext that their bows and arrows and spears were not suitable tools for the task.

Big game hunting by Europeans and Americans emerged as an important source of revenue for Kenya. The business was dominated by white hunters, however; whites were tour operators and guides, Africans were porters, gun bearers, and skinners. A variety of rules and regulations was developed to make it extremely difficult for Africans to cross these divisions, a state of affairs that lasted into the early 1960s.

Resentment of this unfair relationship was further fueled by a decree that outlawed traditional hunting in 1946, bringing the African way of life to an abrupt halt. Local communities had no choice but to continue to engage in some traditional hunting, giving rise to the poaching phenomenon that is rife today.

By the 1970s, it became evident that the combined effect of licensed hunting and poaching was to threaten the survival of the big game species such as elephants, rhinos, and leopards. In 1977, Kenyans from all walks of life and of every shade of color forced the government to declare a complete ban on hunting. In 1978, the commercial trade in wildlife trophies and products was outlawed. Unfortunately, the worldwide demand for African wildlife products continued, and therefore so did poaching.

When hunting was banned, many Kenyans, white and black, found themselves without jobs. The more enterprising of the ex-guides and trackers began to develop another type of tourism—ecotourism. They coined the phrase "Come shooting to Kenya with your camera." Black Kenyans were able to move away from the less important jobs into management and owning their own companies. They promoted the natural beauty of the country—its biodiversity, wildlife, unique ecosystems, breathtaking scenery, and sunny beaches. Specialized tours were developed for bird lovers, botanical expeditions, and many other groups.

Within five years of the ban on hunting, ecotourism was a booming business. It was able to expand so rapidly, in part, because the wildlife tourism infrastructure that had been built up for sports hunting was easily adapted to an infra-

Figure 2.1   *Travelers encounter an African bull elephant cooling off at Zimbabwe's Matusadona Game Reserve on the shores of Lake Kariska.*

structure for nonconsumptive ecotourism. Thousands, then tens of thousands, then, in 1989, 650,000 ecotourists, found Kenya a major wildlife attraction. They spent their money freely—on accommodations, safari clothes and equipment, in-country transport, tour guides, food, and film.

In 1988, tourism became the country's top foreign exchange earner, beating out coffee and tea for the first time. Since agriculture requires substantially greater capital investments than ecotourism, the "gross national benefit" (subtract capital investment from gross income) of ecotourism will continue to be greater in the years to come.

For several years now, Kenya has been earning in excess of USD 350 million in direct and indirect revenues a year from tourism. Kenya plans an aggressive strategy of growth aimed at increasing the number of tourists from current levels of 650,000 to 1 million annually in five years.

This development strategy has the potential to undermine

the very resource on which it is based, however, unless managed carefully. Experience in Kenya and elsewhere has shown that it may be better to focus more on increasing the quality of the ecotourism experience (and thus the amount of money charged for it) rather than increasing the total number of visitors, and perhaps stretching the carrying capacities of fragile ecosystems beyond their limits.

KENYAN ECOTOURISM: HOW IT WORKS

The success of Kenya's tourism efforts, first for sports hunting, and now for ecotourism, has been based on several factors: a unique wildlife resource, an extensive system of national parks and game reserves, and an intensive promotion and investment effort. The sometimes severe problems associated with its efforts, such as environmental degradation and a dwindling wildlife resource, will be discussed in detail later.

In order to protect its unique wildlife resources, a system of wildlife conservation areas was established by the Kenya National Parks Service soon after World War II and strengthened considerably after Kenya became independent in 1963. Some 17,000 square miles, or 8 percent of the national territory, are protected by fifty-two national parks and reserves. A further 3 percent of the country is designated as forest reserve. These protected areas were selected based on how well they represented a cross-section of habitat and wildlife. The ranges currently under protection stretch from the highest mountains in the country (17,000 feet above sea level) to the mangrove forests of the Indian Ocean and marine environments reaching a maximum depth of sixty fathoms.

Most of the protected areas are in the Great Rift Valley, which starts north of the Jordan River and extends as far south as Mozambique and is one of the world's most spectacular natural wonders. Dense wet forests inhabited by majestic crowned eagles, sweeping savannah grasslands, and sparkling inland lakes: these diverse ecosystems are the heritage of the Great Rift Valley, and the Kenya national parks system.

Several years after Kenya made the transition to ecotourism, mainly through the efforts of private individuals, the government saw that it would be in its national interest to experiment with promoting and providing incentives for ecotourism. In 1965, a special department of tourism was created as part of the Ministry of Tourism and Wildlife; its task was to develop a blueprint for the popularization of Kenya as an attractive tourist destination.

Toward that end, it set in motion a highly successful promotional effort that focused on Kenya's exotic scenery and wildlife. Writers and photographers were commissioned to prepare alluring brochures for distribution around the world. Beautiful calendars and postcards depicting Kenya's colorful wildlife were produced and sold in large quantities. Public relations representatives in key sites such as the United States, Canada, Great Britain, and Western Europe were retained to promote Kenya's image in those areas. Later, representatives were hired in Japan, Southeast Asia, Australia, and New Zealand. Tourist officers were posted at Kenyan embassies and trade missions around the world and continue to be today.

The government entered into a dialogue with tour operators and travel agents in an attempt to address divisive issues such as delays of visitors at entry points and visa problems. A Kenya Tourist Advisory Committee was formed to meet regularly on issues that appeared to be threatening the success of ecotourism efforts. Through this process, potential problems were identified and addressed. Immigration matters were discussed openly and steps taken to streamline the process. Financial issues such as tax rebates, export promotion gratuities, and duty-free imports of equipment were also tackled. No subject was deemed too big or too trivial.

Kenya also decided to provide fiscal incentives for the development of ecotourism and an ecotourism infrastructure. In order to finance its efforts, it raised funds and received technical assistance from development agencies in countries such as Great Britain, West Germany, Switzerland, and Italy, in addition to spending funds held in its own treasury. Although ultimately rejected, the idea of nationalizing the industry was considered; instead, they established the Kenya Tourist Development Corporation (KTDC) in 1966.

The new body was given a mandate to finance up-and-coming Kenyan tour operators, travel agents, and hotel owners, and to make money doing so. In the process, the KTDC embarked on a program of buying shares in foreign-owned firms, with the aim of selling them to promising Kenyan entrepreneurs on special terms. This innovative approach to localizing the tourist industry has made it virtually impossible to distinguish between foreign and locally owned tourism firms.

The government continues to offer incentives to foreign investors, however, through the Foreign Investments Act, which guarantees them repatriation of capital and profits. The potential to attract large sums of "bad" money (i.e., that earned from gambling, drugs, prostitution, etc.) is addressed through an investment vetting system that prohibits it.

Major airlines have also been wooed. Practical incentives are offered in the form of tax exemptions for capital investments and taxes only on income (to date, they do not even pay property taxes), to encourage their involvement with game lodge and hotel development, enabling airlines to earn money on two fronts, plane tickets and accommodations.

While ecotourism in Kenya has been a success, the very attraction on which it is based—wildlife—is severely threatened. Mismanagement of the protected areas, illegal hunting, and a low level of local participation and support for conservation are among the reasons why. Since independence, the Kenyan government has launched several major initiatives to tackle these problems. The jury is still out on what the future will bring, but many of the changes appear promising.

MANAGEMENT OF KENYA'S PARKS AND RESERVES

Despite the fact that nature tourism has been a big foreign exchange earner, until recently very little of that money ($7 million of $350 million) was put back into the resource that supports it—the parks system. Parks personnel and guards were underpaid and worked long hours, equipment was lacking, and poaching was rife—in short, the Department of Wildlife Conservation and Management was unable to manage the areas it was charged to protect due to a lack of funding.

In 1989, President Daniel arap Moi moved to address that problem by establishing the parastatal Kenyan Wildlife Service (KWS), which replaced the Department of Wildlife Conservation and Management. The primary role of KWS is to ensure the protection and management of wildlife both inside and outside the protected areas—and to make that wildlife accessible for viewing by tourists and so promote ecotourism. Under the new system, the income and assets associated with the national parks and game reserves are under the jurisdiction of the KWS, and thus can be plowed back into management and conservation. In addition, the KWS can now set the prices charged for park admissions, accommodations, and so forth. (It has raised the rate 125 percent, to Ksh 200 for foreign nationals. Kenyans continue to pay the relatively low rate of Ksh 40, as they otherwise support KWS through taxes.)

The organization is autonomous and is managed by a board of trustees, which is composed of Kenyan nationals from different sectors of the economy. The budget, however, remains subject to public and parliamentary scrutiny, in order to discourage potential abuses.

Each park and reserve is now run as a separate corporate division, responsible for its own income and expenditures. Some will be developed for high-density (minibus) tourism, others will target the high-income individual who wishes to camp in the midst of nature away from crowds, others will be set aside for as little human impact as possible, while still others will serve as multiple-use sites (research, wildlife management, education, etc.). The effect of increased income for the parks can be seen already in the purchase of modern arms and new communications equipment for park guards, along with higher salaries and other benefits.

Parks personnel now receive nine months of paramilitary training and one year of education in wildlife management, and thus are better equipped to deal with the pressures, such as well-armed ivory poachers, on the areas they protect.

Few other parks management agencies, either in Africa or in the rest of the world, enjoy such autonomy and control as the newly created KWS. If managed wisely, success is guaranteed. However, if the new freedoms are abused or poorly managed, the KWS could find itself at loggerheads with other sectors of the economy.

The scars of the neglect inflicted on the parks system in earlier years through lack of financing will take substantial investment, innovation, and time to heal. KWS has been operating for less than a year and has not yet made public its long-term plans. It will have many important issues to address.

One such issue is determining the carrying capacities for Kenya's parks and reserves. The task is complicated by the fact that the carrying capacity of a given area varies from season to season or year to year depending on the amount of rainfall, and the migration habits of wildlife. In addition, the need to maintain Kenya's democratic traditions makes it difficult to deny access or development opportunities to Kenyan nationals. Nevertheless, a determination of the carrying capacities for humans, vehicles, wildlife, domestic animals, and the like must be made and enforced if the protected areas are to be viable over the long term.

Another, even more critical, issue is stopping the illegal hunting of wildlife. The solutions must address both the poaching by the local communities and the slaughter of elephants and rhinos for ivory by professional black marketeers. Fortunately, the KWS will be aided greatly in its work with the latter by the fact that in 1989, the international community of nations signed an agreement to ban ivory imports (CITES). Poaching of elephants has since scaled down dramatically—park wardens are not finding as many carcasses, and many once-thriving ivory shops have closed their doors. However, other southern African nations with thriving elephant populations (e.g., South Africa, Zimbabwe) continue to sell ivory, which provides incentives for poachers to kill elephants in Kenya and smuggle the ivory into these other countries, where it can be sold legally. Consequently, poaching still occurs. The next meeting on this issue will take place in 1992, at which time it is hoped that a solution for the problem will be presented, and the ban implemented in full measure; if this occurs, poaching for ivory should no longer be a problem.

KWS has also greatly strengthened enforcement. In 1988, the rangers were authorized to shoot poachers on sight, and more than seventy poachers have been killed since. Not one has been a Kenyan, however, which implies that poaching is fueled by forces outside Kenya.

LOCAL PARTICIPATION

The Kenyan government has also moved to address the problems associated with the interaction of neighboring local communities with the protected areas.

Many of the local people are so disgruntled with decades of being ignored that today they are the enemies of the parks and national forests. Their anger has its roots in colonialism and the ban on traditional hunting, and in the fact that the wild game living in the parks are allowed to range freely over private lands, competing with domestic animals, using up essential water supplies, and sometimes contributing to soil erosion and degradation. Until recently, the private landowner saw very little monetary return from this public use of his lands.

Local landowners began to feel that their interests were being treated as less important than those of the animals, and that their good-naturedness was being abused. Some began to put up fences to keep wildlife off their property and others used innovative methods to deny water to migrating wildlife. As a result, the number of wild animals declined noticeably in the reserves, and migration patterns were disrupted.

In response, the government recently developed a number of policies aimed at increasing local participation in the development of tourism, providing financial incentives to local communities to protect the neighboring tourism sites, and encouraging domestic tourism in order to build Kenyan support for the parks.

The Kenyan government is providing fiscal incentives to the local communities through a variety of mechanisms. First, it attempts to ensure that local goods and services, as well as local labor, are used by the tourism industry, through a series of specific requirements. Kenyans must be employed on a preferential basis, with the exception of the most senior personnel, whom the investor may appoint as desired. Hotels and lodges are required to keep imported foodstuffs to a minimum, using Kenyan products wherever possible. The visitors are charged a government hotel tax, a training levy charge, and a service charge, all of which accrue to the Kenyan government (a portion trickles down to the local populations) and are in addition to the normal corporate taxes levied by the government each year on the gross trading income.

Local participation and involvement are the keystone of a policy implemented in 1988 after being negotiated with local communities. Following lengthy discussions, it was agreed that each visitor staying in a game lodge overnight would be charged an extra USD 5 that would be allocated to the local peoples. This money is placed into a trust fund to be used by the private land owners in the area. Some tourists visit reserves that do not have game lodges nearby; in this case, a portion of the entry fee will be deposited into the trust fund.

The trust funds are managed by the people themselves under the neutral chairmanship of the district commissioner or the local game warden. In the case of wrongdoing such as misappropriation of funds, or favoritism, an appeal process has been established. If this is also unfruitful, the aggrieved person may take the case to a court of law. No such problems have yet emerged, however. The money in these trust funds is first distributed for community needs such as schools, cattle dips (where cattle are cleaned of ticks and other parasites), and hospitals. Any money that remains is distributed on a pro rata basis among the affected landowners, based on how much land is involved in the program.

This program is still new and as yet has been implemented only in Amboseli and Masai Mara national parks. There are no real data as yet on how well the system is functioning, though local communities now seem more positive about the parks and local poaching appears to be declining. KWS currently is conducting negotiations for similar programs with communities surrounding other reserves.

Domestic tourism is encouraged through substantially reduced pricing, particularly during the rainy season and school holidays. Educational hostels have been built in strategic locations across the country for schoolchildren and members of the popular Kenyan wildlife clubs. Their maintenance and administration are heavily subsidized by the government. Public buses are available for organized local groups, such as schools, churches, or civic groups, to provide inexpensive transportation to these sites.

PRIVATE RESERVES

In some countries, private reserves play a large role in both preserving wildlife and distributing some of the benefits of ecotourism back to the local communities. There are at present relatively few private reserves in existence in Kenya, however. The best known number six in total. The owners of these areas are mainly wealthy foreigners. The reserves are usually part of a working ranch, located on marginal lands used primarily for cattle grazing. Portions of the ranch are devoted to the protection of wildlife, and the cattle are not allowed in those regions. Some of the more sophisticated of the reserves have built high-priced accommodations for the tourist. They all appeal to the well-heeled visitor who wants to avoid the mass tourism found on the state reserves.

In many cases, the operators of these sites claim they are losing money and that they should be supported by the government and exempted from income taxes. However, if they are truly losing money, why do they wish to continue the operation? And if it were truly nonprofitable, why are more and more people opting for this type of land use?

There are no hard data available on tourism at private reserves. There is no government oversight, either, except that wildlife is legally a national asset, so the KWS theoretically could become involved in the management of the wildlife (if hunting were to occur, for example). Currently, the government has no plans to review the issue. The KWS is, however, planning for that eventuality.

CASE STUDY: MASAI MARA/SERENGETI ECOSYSTEM

The spectacular savannah woodlands of the Mara/Serengeti are what many people envision when they think of Africa. This tropical paradise for wildlife straddles the borders of Kenya and Tanzania (see figure 2.2) and is home to zebras, wildebeests, lions, antelopes, hyenas, jackals, African hunting dogs, giraffes, buffaloes, elephants, and many birds of prey. It is also home to several hundred families of Masai, a nomadic people who base their livelihoods on maintaining large herds of cattle.

Many of the 650,000 visitors to Kenya each year feel their tour is incomplete without a trip to see the Mara/Serengeti. However, the ever-increasing numbers of tourists visiting the site have led to a host of environmental problems. Previous mismanagement of the relationship of the Masai to the reserve has also led to environmental damage by Masai-owned livestock and poaching.

Until 1960, when the 750-square-mile Masai Mara County Council Game Reserve was established, the local Masai had access to all the land in the district, and were free to move southward into Tanzania in search of water and grazing when necessary. The creation of the reserve, together with

Figure 2.2   *Masai Mara and Masai Amboseli Reserves in Kenya.*

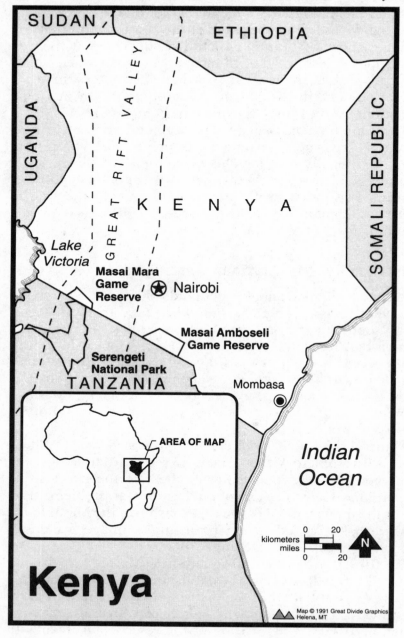

the adjacent Serengeti National Park, which was established a decade earlier, greatly restricted their options without providing any alternatives. In addition, during certain months of the year, the wild game animals forage on the Masai's private lands, competing with Masai livestock and decreasing the productivity of the domestic animals.

In order to address this problem, the government and the Masai agreed on a revenue-sharing scheme (described in greater detail earlier). Each visitor staying in or around the reserve overnight (six lodges are located inside the reserve, seven outside) is charged an extra USD 10 per day, half of which goes to the county council (a local administrative authority). The other half is paid into a trust fund for the local Masai, and managed by them with the help of a locally appointed district commissioner.

As soon as the system was implemented, the shift in community attitudes was immediate and dramatic. The community began to earn a handsome income in excess of nearly USD 1 million a year, and now views wildlife as an asset rather than a liability. Poaching, which had accounted for the loss of tens of thousands of animals annually, dropped to virtually nothing.

Thus, one threat to the future of the reserve has been eliminated—permanently, one hopes. The impact of a virtual avalanche of tourists, however, has yet to be addressed adequately.

The sensitive soils of the savannah are crisscrossed with tire tracks where tourists in search of wildlife have offered drivers large tips to go off the roads. Balloonists swoop over herds of elephants, buffalo, and other animals, causing them to scurry this way and that. (On the other hand, each individual on the balloon pays $250 for a forty-five-minute ride, which makes a strong economic argument in terms of short-term investment criteria for continuing the practice in some form.) The feeding and mating habits of the region's wildlife have been disrupted as animals react to large numbers of viewers. Some animals, such as the cheetahs, become so disturbed that they frequently fail to feed, mate, or raise their young.

The local county council is the richest in the country, but as yet it has not invested enough funds in the development of mechanisms to better control the viewing habits of visitors to the reserves and so alleviate pressures on environmentally sensitive lands. Such an investment would suit its best interests.

Several actions are planned by the Kenyan Wildlife Service that should address the worst of these problems in the Masai Mara and other parks. A first priority is the construction of primary, secondary, and tertiary roads; their use will be mandatory. Road construction is tough on the environment, but the current free-for-all is much worse. A complete ban on the development of additional tourist accommodations or expansion of existing ones is being contemplated. Casual camping will be illegal. Minimum flight levels for balloons, and fixed take-off and landing sites, will be established. Finally, tourists will be asked to be sensitive to the ecological needs of the areas they visit. Without their participation, the environment of the Mara/Serengeti ecosystem will continue to be degraded.

CONCLUSION

Tourism in Kenya has had a stormy history. However, it appears that the government, and to some degree the local communities, has decided that ecotourism is critical to the well-being of the nation and is moving to make it sustainable. The changes in governmental attitudes toward the local people, the increased financial and executive support for the protection of the parks, and the complete ban on the ivory trade have been important steps forward. The future will demonstrate if ecotourism in Kenya will indeed be sustainable, and if it can continue to provide protection for the parks and wildlife of Kenya.

CHAPTER 3

Private Reserves, Parks, and Ecotourism in Costa Rica

YANINA ROVINSKI

Perched on top of the rugged Tilaran Mountain Range in the north of Costa Rica lies Monteverde Cloud Forest Reserve, one of the country's main attractions for natural history lovers (see figure 3.1). This 10,000-hectare private nature reserve hosts a growing flood of tourists who come year after year seeking a glimpse of Monteverde's natural treasures.

The reserve, owned and managed by the Tropical Science Center, is becoming increasingly well known for its wealth of wildlife, its lush green wildlands, and the resplendent quetzal, symbol of freedom and sacred bird of the Mayas. The reserve is also the only home of the brightly colored golden toad. These endangered species, and many other forest dwellers, have turned Monteverde into the tourist attraction it is today. But it was not always this way.

Figure 3.1	*Major nature tourism sites in Costa Rica.*

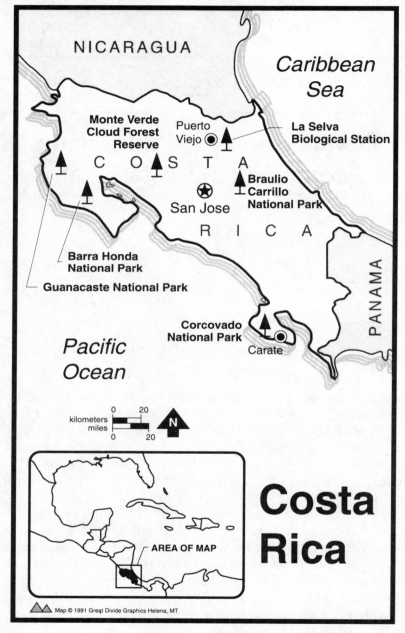

In the early 1950s, Monteverde was mostly untouched primary forest. The cultivated lands ended at the edge of the mountains. The agricultural frontier moved farther up the slopes with time, however, as population increased and laws that favored agricultural expansion were promulgated.

A small community of North American Quakers, seeking peace and a nonviolent way of life, came to settle in these peaceful and isolated Costa Rican mountains in the late 1950s. They bought 1,400 hectares of land, divided it among themselves, and set aside 554 hectares for watershed conservation on the steep slopes of the mountain.

In the 1960s, biologists and students (mostly from the United States) began to visit the protected area, attracted by its rich cloud forest, which was still quite unaltered. They found each tree to be a tropical garden and were able to observe species that were endangered elsewhere. Their research led to the discovery of the golden toad, whose entire habitat lies within a few hectares of Monteverde's dwarf forest.

Interest in preserving this biological wealth against slash-and-burn agriculture began to grow among both the original Quaker settlers, who formed a conservation group called Bosque Eterno, and the Tropical Science Center, a San José–based scientific organization. In 1972, they agreed to found the Monteverde Cloud Forest Reserve.

The number of scientists visiting Monteverde kept increasing. They came to this misty forest, where rain is almost perpetual, to study the habits of bellbirds or photograph umbrella birds. They observed macaws, quetzals, tinamous, agoutis, kinkajous, jaguars, and ocelots. Palms, ferns, mosses, bromeliads, immense oaks, and tiny mushrooms were also studied. Their accounts in technical journals brought other visitors to the area and their studies served as a base for more research. Articles then began to appear in the popular media, attracting visitors who were interested in the beauty of the land or fascinated by its unusual inhabitants.

The number of visitors increased from 300 in 1973 to 15,000 in 1989. The reserve also grew, from 2,000 hectares to 10,000 hectares in 1990.

The large number of visitors has resulted in noticeable changes in the neighboring communities. First, a shelter was built near the reserve. Then, a "pension" and a "soda," which is a type of coffee shop. Today, there are two modern hotels, several guesthouses, a local network of tour guides, a souvenirs and crafts store (which brings in a respectable $50,000 a year), horse rentals, a "cantina," and a disco bar (appropriately called "The Golden Toad").

Changes are also evident within the reserve itself. On the positive side, visitors are bringing substantial income to the reserve, which is used to buy new lands and pay for management of the area. The reserve more than pays for its maintenance with the money from entrance fees (about $2.75 per person) and T-shirt sales. The local economy also benefits from the reserve—tourism is the second largest source of earnings after dairy—which has made Monteverde popular with the local community.

New trails have been built inside, some mainly for tourists, others for research. Unfortunately, erosion on the tourist trails is a growing problem. During the rainy season, the tree roots that border the trails are washed clean and trampled on by the visitors as they walk by. Locals say the habits of the animals are changing and much of the wildlife now stays away from the tourist trails during the high season.

In response, the Monteverde Cloud Forest Reserve group undertook a study of the carrying capacity of the reserve. They found that while the reserve can handle more visitors, the current visitor facilities within the reserve cannot. Their solution is to build a "Monteverde Conservation Center," which will help to educate the ecotourists and groups of Costa Rican students, as well as train Costa Ricans and other Latin Americans as guides. They also plan to build new trails, which will help them better manage the flow of visitors.

Will the increase in tourists mean a decrease in wildlife? Dr. George Powell, one of the founding members of the reserve, thinks not. He has seen a substantial increase in wildlife, especially large mammals, over the last few years. One of his current research projects is examining the impact of tourism on quetzals. His preliminary findings are that the tourists are not disturbing quetzals, unless they molest their nests. This problem can be addressed, he says, by rerouting trails around nests so that tourists will be unable to touch them.

Other questions of overuse related to socioeconomic concerns are also being raised. Visitors wandering onto private lands, changes in the habits of young people who are being influenced by the steadily increasing numbers of tourists, increased costs of living for locals, and the growing pressures on a fragile infrastructure are some of the problems that have emerged.

Monteverde is one of the earliest and best developed examples of a new and thriving industry in Costa Rica: ecotourism.

THE DEVELOPMENT OF ECOTOURISM IN COSTA RICA

The popularity and rapid emergence of ecotourism in Costa Rica is the result of a mixture of circumstances: an astounding and extensively studied biological diversity, sites of extreme natural beauty and easy access, stable political conditions, and an extensive system of protected areas.

The story of ecotourism in Costa Rica is linked closely to that of the national parks. And that story is not very old.

In 1969, some natural resource experts began to lobby for the creation of a system of protected areas in the country. They argued that because most of the forest that originally covered 99.8 percent of Costa Rica had been destroyed, serious steps needed to be taken to preserve at least a small part of that unique heritage. They argued that action needed to be taken right away because every year another 1 percent of the remainder was being cleared by land-hungry farmers and settlers. Resources were disappearing at an alarming rate.

The classic causes of deforestation were responsible: agricultural expansion, timber exploitation, and cattle ranching. At that time, Costa Rica's laws favored agricultural expansion and by the early 1960s, most of the country's exploitable land had an owner. Very often, it was a large landowner. Three-quarters of the agricultural land belonged to 10 percent of the farms. And the big landowners—farmers, ranchers, and loggers—were a powerful lobbying force against the parks.

Costa Rica's conservationists, on the other hand, had compelling arguments and the strong personalities to make them heard. One of the parks' advocates, Mario Boza, fresh out of forestry school, defended his ideas with strong words. Those who opposed the creation of the parks were fools, "absurd people who think forests are meant for logging and nothing else." Confronted with a critical situation, conservationists demanded speedy action. They said that endangered habitats, representative zones, and rich forests had to be protected immediately. There was no time for discussion, no time for philosophical questions. If it was endangered, it needed to be protected.

Park defenders got their way, and the National Parks Service was created in 1970. Twenty years later, almost all the country's natural habitats, from lowland wet forests to high mountain paramos, and from seaside mangroves and swamps to deciduous dry forest, are represented in Costa Rica's thirty-four parks and reserves. The parks now occupy 11 percent of the territory, and most of the dry tropical forests left in the New World are in Costa Rica's protected lands.

The government also has been supportive of the establishment of privately owned reserves for both research and tourism. Monteverde was one of the first, but since then, scores of organizations and individuals have created their own nature reserves. Many border the national parks, which helps them maintain biological diversity, as wildlife can pass between the park and the private reserve. Some actually act as buffer zones for the national parks, diverting both visitor and development pressure.

Unfortunately, deforestation in the rest of Costa Rica continues at a nonsustainable rate, and forestry experts estimate that in less than 10 years, the only exploitable forests remaining will be within the parks and private reserves.

Soon, Costa Rica will see pressure to cut down the protected areas. In response, a new approach to conservation has been adopted in Costa Rica, one that holds much promise for the continued well-being of its wilderness areas.

When the parks were first created, the main priority of the National Parks Service was to preserve habitat. This approach earned enemies among farmers, ranchers, and loggers who wanted to expand their properties and among park dwellers who were relocated and who previously had used the forests as hunting grounds or agricultural land.

The situation grew tense, as the National Parks Service promised future accomplishments and international renown, while the people and other sectors of the government asked for tangible results—meaning income.

In 1986, the government switched responsibility for the National Parks Service and the parks from the Ministry of Agriculture to the recently created Ministry of Natural Resources. The new management had some fresh ideas for the nation's protected areas.

Alvaro Umaña, then minister of natural resources, began to promote a new concept to solve the conservation-versus-development dilemma: sustainable development. Umana introduced alternative schemes for development that would not deplete the country's natural resource base. He refused to accept that, being a country of forest and rivers, Costa Rica would have to suffer from water shortages and deforestation.

And thus began the talk of development schemes within a conservationist framework. More intensive production techniques for farming were called for to lower the need for agricultural expansion. Parks and reserves were to be managed for sustainable development and grouped in regional megaparks, with the neighboring communities viewed as "areas of influence." The use of protected areas for lucrative and nondestructive activities, such as ecotourism, became a priority.

That is how a small number of private entrepreneurs who had already put their money on ecotourism found support among conservationists.

It was not a bad idea, conservationists said, to convince private investors to put their money into conservation. People would be more likely to protect the areas where their financial interests were at stake. And a campaign was launched to convince investors that conservation could be a lucrative business. The war-horse of this campaign was ecotourism.

HOW PRIVATE ENTERPRISE MET NATURE TOURISM

The Costa Rican government, while it had the best of intentions, lacked the funds to develop national parks and protected areas for ecotourism. There was no money for visitor facilities, no money for training guides and interpreters, and very little money for basic management. If ecotourists were to be satisfied with their trips to Costa Rica, these had to be provided. So the private sector was presented with a unique opportunity—the government would provide the natural resources if the private sector would provide the services; and the private sector would reap most of the financial benefits.

COSTA RICA EXPEDITIONS

Michael Kaye arrived in Costa Rica in 1978 with plans to open a travel agency that specialized in river rafting. On his first visit to Costa Rica several years before, he had found good rafting rivers, rough, exciting, and unspoiled, and as a river-rafting enthusiast, he thought there would be a market for selling river-rafting tours to North Americans.

He was right. Clients came in droves for the rivers. What he hadn't foreseen is that they would return for the wilderness. Kaye saw requests for wilderness excursions piling up on his desk and slowly began to shift from rafting to "off-the-beaten-track" excursions, as his Costa Rica Expeditions Travel Agency now advertises.

Today, 75 percent of Kaye's clients come for natural history tours and excursions. He brings in about 20,000 clients a year, and each one spends an average of $148 a day. His ecotourism agency is currently the largest ecotourism agency in the country, but others are hot on its trail. Kaye employs Costa Ricans as managers and guides, though most are not from the rural communities near where he runs tours.

Costa Rican Ecotour Operators Proliferate

While Kaye, an American, was the first in-country operator to focus exclusively on ecotourism, the ecotourism business is now dominated by Costa Ricans. Shortly after Kaye opened his doors. Tikal, which had already established itself as a general tourism agency, decided that the natural history market held great promise, and coined the term "ecotourism" in its brightly illustrated brochures of Costa Rica's natural attractions. And Horizontes, the brainchild of two young Costa Rican entrepreneurs, was created to cater to scientists, students, and other nature lovers.

Tamara Budowski and Margarita Forero, owners of Horizontes, carefully planned the enterprise to serve the purpose of leading naturalists to the country's most attractive wildernesses. Budowski (a native Costa Rican) grew up in Switzerland, where she became accustomed to beautiful landscapes but was astonished by its lack of wildlife when she returned to Costa Rica as a teenager: she had never seen fish in the rivers of Switzerland, nor the variety of wildlife she found in the unspoiled tropical lands.

Budowski and Forero financed their idea by selling tickets for trips abroad to Costa Ricans. The profit went to fund an agency that organized nature tours. As the agency grew, it moved away from ticket sales and is now solely dedicated to its original purpose: ecotourism in Costa Rica.

In two or three years, over a dozen new agencies were created. Coming from diverse backgrounds, businessmen, biologists, conservationists, and traditional tour operators began to make their way toward the ecotourism market.

As these agencies promoted their country's attractions, the growing flow of visitors began to create a need for simple

Figure 3.2   *Biologists and students were the main visitors to nature reserves during the early years. They still come in considerable numbers.*

PHOTO: Yanina Rovinski

accommodations near such parks as Corcovado, Braulio Carrillo, and Monteverde. In just a few years, operators and other investors created lodges and shelters for ecotourists around the country. This basic infrastructure allowed tour operators to lead groups to some of the country's most beautiful protected lands, providing visitors comfort or at least the opportunity to sleep on dry, clean sheets after a day's adventurous trekking through the forest.

Sergio Miranda and his family own a plot of land at the edge of the Corcovado National Park. During weekends spent at their farm, Miranda met scientists who complained about the harsh living conditions at Corcovado's shelters and the difficulties of obtaining transportation to and from the area.

He thought he could provide a new means of transportation and some basic accommodations on the farm as a hobby, but during a market research tour in the United States, Miranda discovered that instead of attracting scientists, he aroused the interest of travel agents. Thus was created Marenco, today one of Costa Rica's best-known ecotourism resorts.

Almost at the same time, Amos Bien, a tropical biologist who had been working with the Organization for Tropical Studies (OTS) and other research institutions in Costa Rica, decided attention needed to be focused on the 90 percent of the country's lands that were not under legal protection as national parks.

Bien believed that deforestation occurred due to economic needs, and therefore the solutions needed to be financial. He then purchased a natural area he named Rara Avis, an experiment on "rain forest conservation for profit."

Ecotourism is the foremost activity of the private reserve, though sustainable forestry and alternative forest crops such as ornamental plants are also under way. Bien's tourism activities at the edge of Braulio Carrillo National Park cause about $80,000 to accrue to the local community annually, which makes ecotourism one of the most important sources of income and employment for the neighboring settlement of Horquetas.

A CASE STUDY: PLACING COSTA RICA ON THE NATURALIST'S MAP

The growth of ecotourism in Costa Rica has been greatly facilitated by the presence of the Organization for Tropical Studies. Although OTS was neither a commercial travel agency nor a conservation organization, it was responsible for helping to create Costa Rica's image abroad as a tropical paradise through bringing tens of thousands of visitors to the country.

Created in 1963, the North Carolina–based international consortium of universities and research institutions owns three research sites in Costa Rica: the La Selva and Palo Verde Biological Field Stations and the Robert and Catherine Wilson Botanical Garden. These function as open-air classrooms and laboratories for tropical science students and professionals, providing hands-on experience for members of OTS's forty-eight member institutions.

More than 2,500 biology students have embarked on their first studies of tropical ecology at one of OTS's field stations; many have written and published papers resulting from their research work there; and most tropical scientists working in the New World today have at some point studied or worked at OTS.

When space permits, groups of nonacademic visitors also visit La Selva to see birds, frogs, and insects, as well as its unique vegetation.

Were OTS a profit-making institution, it would be Costa Rica's most successful travel agency, with La Selva its main resort. All the students and scientists OTS brings to the country need to be housed, fed, and provided with guides. And the number arriving each year keeps increasing, surpassing 20,000 person-days at La Selva in 1989 (a combined measure of number of visitors and time spent in the place).

But the direct financial impact of OTS-related ecotourism only represents a small part of the organization's overall effect on the industry. It is the research and publications generated through OTS that has put Costa Rica on the map of the ecotourist—especially scientists, but many other types of nature lovers as well.

LA SELVA BIOLOGICAL STATION

La Selva Biological Field Station is near Puerto Viejo in Sarapiquí, a two-hour drive from San José. The newly paved road crosses the central mountain range, then drops abruptly toward the Atlantic lowlands of northeastern Costa Rica. The vegetation change is dramatic. In less than fifteen minutes, mountain cypresses and moss-covered oaks with more orchids and bromeliads than a fancy flower shop are replaced by white-flowered lilies and tree ferns, and by achiote shrubs and African and peach palm trees a little farther on. Its long-term viability and diversity is assured by the fact that it abuts the immense Braulio Carrillo National Park, allowing wildlife to travel to and from the station.

At first sight, the station does not appear to be a tropical jungle, as its Spanish name, La Selva (The Jungle), indicates. The entrance leads to a recently acquired pasture with modern barracks, housing cabins, a dining room, and a laundry room. Each room is a tidy cabin with bunk beds, bathroom, running water, and electricity. Visitors are greeted with clean sheets and instruction leaflets, a map of the station, and registration forms.

But on crossing the hanging bridge that separates the pasture from the old La Selva, and walking past the modern laboratories that house sophisticated equipment for chemical analysis, geographical information systems, and biological research, one suddenly reaches the real La Selva: 2,000 acres of virgin forest, swamps, and abandoned plantations.

Until 1968, La Selva belonged to ecologist Leslie Holdrige, who had planned to turn it into a commercial forest and fruit farm. He planted cacao and pejibaye (peach palm) for fruits, and laurel for wood, but more than 85 percent of the land was preserved as virgin forest.

When OTS bought the farm, the plantations were abandoned. A small plot was transformed into an arboretum that bears Holdrige's name. The plot includes more than 1,000 trees with 240 species represented—two-thirds of La Selva's total. The farm also includes secondary forest, pastures, and experimental plots. But most of it is virgin forest: a real jungle with swamps and caymans, lianas and strangler vines, innumerable dwarf palms, and endless varieties of birds.

During its early years, La Selva's visitors were mostly North American students, and most research remained the property of "ivory tower" scientists. This changed with time. Courses in Spanish attracted and trained national and regional biologists and naturalists. Publications in both English and Spanish began to increase La Selva's popularity as a research station. The wild beauty of the station became apparent as less technical articles were published, and interest began to grow among nonspecialists as well—birdwatchers in particular.

About 60 percent of OTS visitors return, and some 69 percent persuade others to visit as well. The expenditures that have accrued to Costa Rica because of OTS return travel (up through 1987) are about $7.51 million (Laarman 1987). Today, 13,000 nature tourists visit La Selva each year, spending $291,000 in 1989.

REGULATION OF ECOTOURISM

The spectacular growth in the ecotourism industry has had a downside. Conservationists and operators, to a lesser degree, are concerned that uncontrolled ecotourism will destroy the very resource upon which it is based. One of the most popular beachfront parks, Manuel Antonio, is experiencing overcrowding, water pollution, trail erosion, and disrupted wildlife behavior. Monteverde, which has received the most international press, is virtually overwhelmed with visitors at the peak season. Wildlife at the Carrara National Park has been molested by tourists who walk in unaccompanied by a guide, even though they are required to have one.

Misuse of the park's resources by the neighboring communities is another problem, one that has not yet been adequately addressed by tour operators or the government. It is common to see small homesteads carved into the sides of the national parks, trees cut down within park limits, and exotic wildlife poached for sale to the North or for food on the table. Each national park includes an environmental education component in its management plan that is supposed to engender community support.

However, with a few exceptions such as Braulio Carrillo National Park and Guanacaste National Park, these programs have not been very successful. In Braulio Carrillo, park managers have organized local communities to take advantage of the income possibilities presented by ecotourism, and in Guanacaste, managers have hired local citizens to help manage the park, as well as initiated extensive environmental education programs.

In response to abuses by operators and tourists, informal regulations regarding the conduct of tours have started to emerge. Nature-oriented tours are to be led by biologists or other natural history experts. Groups must be kept small and manageable. Carrying capacity has to be respected for protected areas. Accommodations should be built at a considerable distance from parks and reserves, and money has to be spent as close to the wildlands as possible, in order to engender local support.

Some of these regulations are being respected. But for the most part, compliance is self-monitored. And ecotourism continues to grow without planning or oversight.

General tourism in Costa Rica is regulated by the legal arm of the National Tourism Board (ICT), itself a part of the Ministry of Industry and Commerce. ICT is a mammoth institution, dealing with such varied tourism issues as transportation, infrastructure, foreign investment, advertising, zoning, and regulation. On first glance, it would seem clear that ICT should provide regulations for nature tourism, as part of its other tourism activities.

On closer look, the issue becomes more complicated. National legislation has put the regulation of all activities dealing with protected areas under the responsibility of the Ministry of Natural Resources, Energy, and Mines.

The ministry acknowledges the need to regulate parks visitation, but states that each area must define its own regulations in its management plan, taking into consideration such variables as carrying capacity and work priorities. Such management plans exist in only a few parks, and are being implemented in just a handful. Visitor regulations, if they exist, generally address simple issues, such as alcohol consumption, entrance of pets, use of portable stereos and footballs, and extraction of plants and wildlife. The carrying capacity of the sites is seldom determined.

Visitor services (which could help control the negative impacts of visitation) are also lacking. Parks personnel are rarely trained, even to the extent of providing basic guidance and information services. Interpretation trails exist in only a few of the most developed parks. Information for the visitor is next to nonexistent, and the Parks Service has a budget that barely pays survival salaries to the existing personnel. This budget has not been increased in nearly ten years due to the freeze imposed on governmental growth by international financing institutions, and to the fact that park entrance fees, which are kept extremely low for Costa Ricans, are not raised for the foreign visitor who can afford to pay a good deal more.

The National Tourism Board sees clearly that the growing number of visitors attracted by protected areas presents an opportunity for economic growth. Tourism in general is the third largest foreign exchange earner in the country (after coffee and bananas) and brought in $132.7 million in 1986. According to recent visitor surveys, about 36 percent specifically cite ecotourism as among their main reasons for visiting Costa Rica (Boo 1990).

Yet ecotourism is not a priority in ICT's budget. Tourism officials assume that through promoting the country as a general tourism destination (emphasizing beaches, hotels, etc.), ecotourism will indirectly benefit. Encouraging large-scale tourism, huge beach developments, and providing foreign investment packages are the board's main priorities.

Incentives provided for tourism investment by ICT rarely

apply to the small kinds of development needed for nature tourism. Paperwork is sometimes so complicated that small investors shy away. And regulations on guides and transportation services are generally not appropriate for ecotourism.

Tourism officials claim the main responsibility for regulation lies with conservationists and that development should be conducted by the private sector. They have not yet clarified what ICT's role should be, but it appears clear that it will remain on the sidelines.

Private entrepreneurs consider this a mistake, since the number of visitors coming to the country for nature-oriented activities has been growing steadily, to reach almost 40 percent of all tourists (the total number of tourists in 1989 was 375,951). Such numbers, they argue, make it clear that nature tourism should be a priority of the Tourism Board.

Conservation officials also state that much of nature tourism should be regulated by the Tourism Board, though they have developed some minor regulations related to usage of trails, extraction of natural resources, and hours of visitation. On issues such as appropriately trained guides and investment and regulation for tourism infrastructure near the parks, neither the National Parks Service nor the National Tourism Board is willing to take responsibility.

In an attempt to address this problem, a special cooperative board on ecotourism was founded in March of 1990. Its members included representatives from private enterprise, the Parks Service, the National Tourism Board, and other institutions. No action was taken at the meeting, however, and the next meeting has yet to be called. Most were agreed that if the new board were to function, funds would have to be found to hire someone to coordinate the effort.

THE BOOM: PRESENT STATE OF THE INDUSTRY

By 1990, ten years after the first ecotourism agency was created in Costa Rica, the number of enterprises dealing with nature-oriented visitors had reached unexpected propor-

tions. More than twenty specialized agencies were functioning, nature shelters and resorts had opened throughout the
country, and guide-training facilities were being developed.

The real "boom," according to private entrepreneurs, has
occurred in the last three years, after the image of Costa Rica
was projected around the world by two events: the Seven-
teenth General Assembly of the World Conservation Union,
held in San José in 1988, where the country's record of ac-
complishment in conservation was made public; and the
award of the Nobel Peace Prize to Costa Rica's president Os-
car Arias in 1987 for his efforts to create peace in Central
America, thereby ridding the country of the widespread image of Central American "banana republics," haunted by
wars and dictatorships.

Since then, the number of visitors coming to Costa Rica
has been on a steady incline. The need for such facilities as
shelters, guides, transportation, interpreters, equipment
rentals, tourism operators, and managers is also increasing.
Hotels are now full most of the year. Hot spots such as Monteverde do not have a low tourism season anymore.

Ecological tourism centers are sprouting up everywhere,
and those already in existence are considering expansion
and diversification.

A graduate course on ecotourism has been created by a
private university to prepare naturalist guides, tour operation managers, and supervisors for entrance into this growing field.

Souvenir shops have filled up with nature books, posters,
and maps. Colorful ceramic birds are replacing the typical
painted oxcarts as favorite souvenirs. Postcards feature nature instead of churches. And the prefix "eco" is featured in
almost any ad dealing with tourism these days. When Costa
Ricans want to sell something, they paint it green.

International funding agencies, both those interested in
development and those dealing with conservation, are
studying and funding nature tourism activities.

This enthusiasm is mostly considered positive by conservationists, yet some warnings are already being heard. Foremost is the fact that carrying capacity should not be

surpassed. Conservationists point out that a park is like a movie theater: if its capacity is 150, visitor 151 will not fit in and will endanger the security of the others. Yet the carrying capacities of most parks have yet to be determined.

Another important consideration is the distribution of the benefits. One of conservationists' basic reasons to support nature tourism is the need to provide alternative sources of income to park neighbors, to avoid their coveting the land for agriculture, hunting, logging, or other such activities. If economic benefits do not reach local populations, the battle for conservation will be lost.

The need for well-trained personnel, to provide both security and information to the visitors, is also growing among those in charge of protected areas.

Tourism infrastructure near the parks has been expanding, although regulations and proper incentives do not yet exist. This development could get out of hand unless speedy measures are taken.

Ecotourism is based on a fragile and limited resource: protected natural ecosystems. Unregulated and excessive ecotourism ultimately will destroy itself. Yet efforts to plan and manage ecotourism in Costa Rica are still in the early stages. More research and regulation are needed soon if this new industry is to achieve its potential.

REFERENCES

Boo, Elizabeth. 1990. *Ecotourism: The Potentials and Pitfalls.* Vol. 2. Washington, D.C.: World Wildlife Fund-U.S.

Laarman, Jan. 1987. "A Survey of Return Visits to Costa Rica by OTS Participants and Associates." Working paper. Raleigh: North Carolina State University.

CHAPTER 4

Tourism in Greater Yellowstone: Maximizing the Good, Minimizing the Bad, Eliminating the Ugly

DENNIS GLICK

S ome hail tourism as a panacea that will cure the eco-nomic woes of the sprawling 14-million-acre Greater Yellowstone Ecosystem. Others warn tourism could be a Trojan horse that will disgorge all manner of ecological and social chaos on this spectacular region. Yet despite these varied opinions, nearly everyone agrees that tourism in Greater Yellowstone will exert increasing influence on the area's economic, environmental, and social systems. Concerned conservationists are taking a hard look at this emerging industry and its impacts on Greater Yellowstone, and are planning for its future.

AN ECOSYSTEM PROFILE

From outer space, the Greater Yellowstone Ecosystem appears on a satellite image as a vast island of mountains and plateaus, rising from the high plains to form one of the most extensive tracts of wildlands in the lower forty-eight states (see figure 4.1). Straddling the tri-state area of Wyoming, Montana, and Idaho, the Ecosystem encompasses two national parks (Yellowstone and Grand Teton), portions of seven national forests, three national wildlife refuges, Bureau of Land Management lands, and state and private properties.

The region boasts the world's most extensive array of geysers and geothermal features, some of North America's largest herds of elk, bison, and bighorn sheep, over 300 species of birds (nearly half of those found in the United States), and several threatened and endangered plants and animals ranging from the diminutive Yellow Spring Beauty to the majestic grizzly bear.

Perhaps even more significant, Greater Yellowstone represents one of the largest, essentially intact temperate zone ecosystems on earth. It is a resource of national and international importance. Created in 1872, Yellowstone National Park was both the birthplace of the national park movement and one of the first areas listed on the United Nations' registry of World Heritage Sites.

This combination of spectacular scenery, readily visible big game, wondrous geothermal features, nearly unsurpassed outdoor recreation opportunities, and unique history draws nearly 10 million tourists annually to the public lands of the Ecosystem. The majority of these visitors are "nature tourists," that is, they are touring relatively undisturbed natural areas with the specific objective of admiring, studying, and enjoying the scenery and its flora and fauna. Indeed, a survey by the Montana Department of Tourism revealed that over three-quarters of all out-of-state tourists reportedly visit national parks while vacationing, and that over 90 per-

Figure 4.1   *Recreation sites in the Greater Yellowstone Ecosystem.*

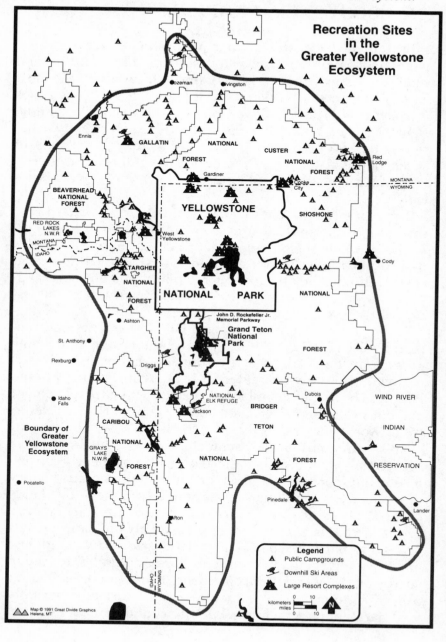

cent of those rated Montana as a "good" or "excellent" place to enjoy outdoor recreation (Brock et al. 1990).

Nature-oriented tourists, however, are not only from outside the region. In 1985, the percentage of Idaho, Montana, and Wyoming residents who participated in "nonconsumptive" wildlife-related activities (observing or photographing) was nearly the highest in the nation. Yellowstone Park, for instance, reported that 19 percent of its visitors in July of 1989 were from Wyoming, Idaho, and Montana and that during the off-season, the percentage of regional visitors doubled (Brandt 1990). The Wyoming Recreation Commission found that "the most active participants in backpacking [in Wyoming] are typically lifelong residents of Wyoming" (Wyoming Recreation Commission 1985).

Greater Yellowstone tourism statistics compiled by government agencies seem to indicate a general leveling off of annual visitation, though a significant shift in seasonality has been observed. In 1967, for example, around 5,200 travelers braved the harsh winter weather of Yellowstone Park to explore the region during this formerly tranquil "off-season." By 1988, that number had skyrocketed to 71,000 (Yellowstone National Park 1990). The implications of this shift affect not only the local economies, but also the health of wildlife and natural habitats.

The accuracy of these visitor counts are, however, somewhat suspect, particularly when one considers the finding that the overall number of visitors has remained stable. One researcher described a recreation estimation procedure commonly used by the Forest Service in the Pacific Northwest as the "SWAG" Method—"Scientific Wild Ass Guess" (Kocis 1986). Research methodologies vary widely among the resource management agencies due to a lack of communication and coordination, though some agencies are starting to increase cooperation on research and investigations.

It is difficult to project just what the future holds for the tourism industry in the region. Projections of trends in tourism generally are based on four fueling factors: population, income, travel patterns, and amount of leisure time. However, in the case of nature tourism, a fifth factor, the ecological condition of the wildland resource, should be added.

Nature tourists want to see nature, not degraded landscapes or depleted wildlife populations. As the cumulative impacts of a host of development activities, such as logging, mining, oil and gas development, and urbanization, whittle away at Greater Yellowstone's natural attractions, the possibility for increasing or even maintaining tourism numbers could be in jeopardy. Already forests and natural habitats have been fragmented, wildlife migratory routes disrupted, and important ecosystem processes and components eliminated or severely altered.

Further complicating the situation is the fact that this vast region with its complex ecological interrelationships is managed by twenty-seven different agencies, including the National Park Service, the Fish and Wildlife Service, the Forest Service, the Bureau of Land Management, and three state fish and wildlife services. These agencies often have conflicting management objectives—the Park Service wants to manage the area for preservation, the Forest Service for timber, for example.

Resource protection in Greater Yellowstone is required not only to maintain biodiversity, but also to protect the natural features that attract tourists. Nations around the world are accelerating efforts to establish and develop parks and opportunities for the nature tourist. With increasing mobility and affluence, the choices for travelers interested in natural history continue to expand. Older, well-established parks and reserves must now compete with the more recently protected natural wonders of other regions and nations. The tourism market is a global market, with nature-tourism-related opportunities and activities in one region affecting those in another. But as long as its unique combination of biological and geological features is preserved, Greater Yellowstone can be expected to continue to receive large numbers of regional, national, and international visitors.

What will be the impact of this flow of humanity on both the environmental and socioeconomic characteristics of

Greater Yellowstone? A 1985 report prepared for the Wyoming Futures Project—which was an attempt to plan for an economically viable future for Wyoming—stated that "this industry [tourism] can have significant economic and cultural advantages for Wyoming, it must be further developed [through improved marketing]" (Public Policy Center 1985). But there is, as the saying goes, no such thing as a free lunch. How much will such a banquet cost the environment and the people of Greater Yellowstone?

THE GOOD

There is no doubt that the direct and indirect benefits of tourism have been impressive and far-reaching in the case of Greater Yellowstone. In fact, Joseph Sax, author of *Mountains Without Handrails,* cites evidence that the impetus for the establishment of Yellowstone and several other national parks came from the lobbying efforts of early tourism promoters. Sax notes that while the popular account of the founding of Yellowstone "holds that the idea for the park was conceived by one of the early exploratory parties," in fact, "an agent for the Northern Pacific Railroad Company, passed on to Washington a suggestion . . . 'Let Congress pass a bill reserving the Great Geyser Basin as a public park forever' . . . Subsequently the Northern Pacific became the principal means of access to Yellowstone and its first concessionaire providing services for tourists."

Tourism officials today, concerned about maintaining the natural attractions that are drawing tourists, are encouraging other state and federal agencies to preserve wildland areas. Sandra Guedes, of the "Travel Montana" office in Montana's Department of Commerce, foresees "increasing cooperation between tourism promoters and organizations whose mandate is the protection of natural resources." This seems only appropriate for an agency that has adopted the slogan "Montana: Unspoiled, unforgettable."

Yellowstone National Park is on the short list of natural icons considered a "must see" by the American public, and is one of the most heavily visited parks in the system. Past and present visitors to Greater Yellowstone have become the Ecosystem's staunchest defenders and many have become active conservationists. Thus, ecotourism to the park plays an important educational role and is largely responsible for the fact that there is a sizable national and even international constituency lobbying for its protection.

Nature tourism is not only important due to its educational and conservation potential, of course. The associated economic benefits provide incentive for people to manage the resource for nature tourism.

In Greater Yellowstone, direct economic impacts at the regional level are difficult to assess. Indirect impacts—goods and services purchased by businesses serving the tourism market—are even more problematic. Still, increasingly sophisticated studies are providing some measure of tourist expenditures and contribution to local economies.

In the state of Montana, for example, nonresident travelers spent approximately $658 million in direct expenditures (lodging, travel, food, etc.) in 1989, according to the Institute for Tourism and Recreation Research. Travelers to Wyoming spent $700 million in 1982 (Public Policy Center 1985).

In a report prepared for Congress, the U.S. Congressional Research Service found that "recreation supports more employment than any other activity in the National Forests of Greater Yellowstone, and except for phosphate mining in the Caribou National Forest, is responsible for two thirds of the jobs resulting from all activities in the National Forests." In the Montana portion of the Ecosystem, the estimated expenditures of nonresident travelers in 1988 was $140 million and total economic impact generated was nearly $250 million, according to the University of Montana. The same report stated that regional tourism generated 5,800 jobs (Institute for Tourism and Recreation Research 1989).

In Wyoming, the county that had the lowest unemployment rate in 1988 was Teton, gateway to Grand Teton National Park and considered by some as the "tourism mecca" of the Ecosystem. The economic impact of tourism in the Idaho portion of the Ecosystem is considerably less (its portion of the ecosystem is smaller, and the area around it more degraded), but, according to the Idaho Department of Commerce, "the communities of Fremont and Teton counties possess a tremendous opportunity to enhance tourism services and destinations that will add to the attractions of the Yellowstone/Grand Teton Complex" (Idaho Department of Commerce 1989). The development of tourism in eastern Idaho will undoubtedly increase visitation and length of stay in this corner of the Ecosystem.

Tourism-related jobs are often stereotyped as low-paying and of short duration. Tourism promoters argue that these jobs provide entry-level opportunities for new additions to the work force and for people in need of employment. In addition, the work is often sought after by students and others wishing part-time positions, due to their seasonal nature.

Tourism proponents point out that many of these jobs are, in fact, well-paying professional positions. The industry requires a host of skilled personnel, ranging from managers and administrators to computer specialists and accountants. In addition, a large percentage of tourism expenditures (28 percent in Montana in 1989) goes directly to retail sales, and not only restaurants and lodging (Institute for Tourism and Recreation Research 1989).

THE BAD AND THE UGLY

"Tourism destroys tourism," reported the Organization for Economic Cooperation and Development in 1980 (Boo 1990). In the Greater Yellowstone Ecosystem, the actions of tourists have degraded fragile resources and, in some cases, caused irreparable environmental damage. Minute and Ebony geysers, at the Norris Geyser Basin in Yellowstone Park, have ceased erupting because of litter carelessly tossed in their mouths. Near Old Faithful, the brilliant colors of the Morning Glory pool have faded due to a lowering of water temperature after garbage plugged its vent.

Other site-specific impacts of tourism include the trampling of vegetation, noise pollution, litter, and water pollu-

Figure 4.2 *Bison and snowmobilers interact in Yellowstone National Park.*

PHOTO: *Jackson Hole News*

tion. *Giardia* has become rampant throughout the waters of the ecosystem, solely due to the activities of outdoor recreationists. Forest fires have been started by careless campers who have also stripped areas of firewood, disrupting natural processes. Some poaching is attributed to tourists, and the introduction of exotic species for fishermen and hunters, such as eastern brook trout, has wreaked havoc on native animal populations. Clearly, these actions are placing a heavy burden on the resources of Greater Yellowstone.

In addition to these obvious problems, other, more subtle environmental modifications are also having a significant cumulative impact. For example, in January of 1990, a lone cross-country skier was attacked by a coyote near Old Faithful. This was the climax of several episodes of emboldened coyotes threatening park visitors. Upon closer investigation, it was discovered that tourists had been accustoming coyotes to human handouts, inadvertently signing the coyotes' death warrants (they were shot by the Park Service). Uninformed tourists continue to feed the coyotes, however, and the animals have now replaced bears as Yellowstone's most common roadside beggars.

In 1978, Congress required that the National Park Service establish a visitor carrying capacity for each unit of the national park system. The National Parks and Conservation Foundation, which has been assisting the Park Service in developing a management process for evaluating and managing visitor use in the parks, reports that "the National Park Service's response to these calls for controls has been scattered and inconsistent" (National Parks and Conservation Foundation 1988).

Many national parks, including Yellowstone, are being managed according to outdated management plans that do not take into account new stresses on the ecosystem. For example, the Park Service developed a detailed plan for winter use in Yellowstone, through upgrading visitor facilities, before they prepared an environmental impact assessment. A recently released "Winter Use Plan Environmental Assessment" does nothing of the sort, but is a general policy document that says the Service will develop a "visitor use management process" (Yellowstone National Park 1990).

Though the era of blatant commercialization of the parks seems to be on the wane, a significant portion of the area has been developed for hotels and other types of concessions. The construction of this infrastructure has had major environmental impacts, as has the increased visitor use due to their presence.

Tourism is also changing the nature of many communities bordering the Ecosystem. In some cases, the impact has been positive. Efforts to develop a thriving tourism industry were responsible for impressive restoration of buildings and infrastructure improvements in West Yellowstone and the development of the widely acclaimed Buffalo Bill museum in Cody. But efforts to capture tourist dollars have also resulted in numerous ill-planned and environmentally unsound developments. Billboards, garish signs, and other tourist "lures" increasingly clutter the otherwise magnificent landscapes of Paradise Valley in Montana and Jackson Hole, Wyoming, among other sites.

Research on the negative socioeconomic impacts of tour- ism generally focuses on so-called fragile or exotic cultures, especially those of the Third World. But it is evident that the social, cultural, and economic makeup of rural American communities can also be turned topsy-turvy by poorly man- aged tourism. Traffic jams in former one-horse towns, soar- ing land prices, sprawling development gobbling up precious greenery, deteriorating air quality, these are the all- too-common trappings of the modern "tourist town."

While these problems relate directly to the activities of tourists, it is often the indirect impacts of tourism—the con- struction of visitor facilities, roads, parking lots, trails, and other tourism-related infrastructure—that cause the most damage to supposedly "protected wildlands." Termed "in- dustrial tourism" by writer Edward Abbey, and a "recreation trap" by conservationist Joyce Kelley (Kutay 1989), many believe that tourism threatens to swap many of the nation's crown jewels for dime store baubles.

The saga of the Fishing Bridge Campground and Visitor's Center in Yellowstone National Park is one of the most ob- vious examples of a tourism facility that has had a devastat- ing impact on a precious living resource, the grizzly bear. As its name would imply, Fishing Bridge is a favorite fishing site for both humans and bears. The inevitable conflicts between the two breeds of fishermen have resulted in the death or removal of more grizzlies than in any other site in the Eco- system.

In an effort to resolve the problem, it was proposed that a new recreational facility be developed in West Thumb on Yellowstone Lake, where grizzlies are less common, and Fishing Bridge be closed to humans. However, some local residents, concerned about the possible diversion of tourist traffic from their city to other gateway communities, lobbied against its closure. Fishing Bridge is still operating, albeit with some new, bear-related restrictions, *and* a new, sprawl- ing complex of stores, restaurants, lodging, and other struc- tures has been built. Fortunately, improved management has led to less conflict with the grizzlies, and the situation appears to be improving.

MAXIMIZING THE GOOD, MINIMIZING THE BAD

It is possible to maximize the positive economic, environmental, and social impacts of tourism in Greater Yellowstone, and reduce or eliminate the negative. Tourism projects, especially those with a "nature tourism" orientation, are becoming a standard component of efforts to establish sustainable economies in areas adjacent to protected wildlands around the world. "We see the possibility for a much stronger alliance between tourism and conservation," says Jim Thorsell, director of the Parks Commission of the International Union for the Conservation of Nature (IUCN) (Kutay 1989).

In Greater Yellowstone, the economic contribution of the service-oriented sector of the economy, which includes tourism, has far surpassed that of the extractive industries (timber, mining, oil and gas development). However, there is growing concern that the rapid expansion of tourism could threaten the conservation gains associated with the curtailment of the more blatantly destructive land use practices.

"Proactive" efforts to plan tourism so that it meets both economic and conservation goals are under way in the Ecosystem. These are being carried out by federal, state, and local government agencies, as well as by private organizations and concerned citizens.

The Greater Yellowstone Coalition, a conservation group dedicated to protecting the ecological integrity of the region and promoting an "ecosystem approach" to resource management, has launched an ambitious effort to develop a blueprint for the long-term protection of the Ecosystem. Part of the first phase of this project, titled "Greater Yellowstone Tomorrow," is taking a close look at the environmental and economic impacts of tourism. In the second phase, recommendations for environmentally sensitive development in the region, including nature-based tourism, will be presented. These will form part of a comprehensive set of resource management guidelines that must be implemented if the wilderness qualities of Greater Yellowstone are to be preserved. An important component of the project is a collaborative effort with several Ecosystem communities to begin to build economies that are based on a sustainable approach to development.

The federal government's Greater Yellowstone Coordinating Committee (GYCC), which is formulating an Ecosystemwide set of management goals and "implementing criteria" to govern National Park Service and Forest Service activities, has included several goals that relate directly to outdoor recreation and tourism. For example, the committee's philosophy statement calls for protecting "the sense of naturalness," and explains that the achievement of this goal "implies that management recognizes the worth of this ecologically unified area as a source of education, recreation and inspiration" (GYCC 1989).

At the site-specific level, the Park Service has initiated work on a winter use plan and environmental assessment for Yellowstone Park. This long overdue study will detail plans for developing and managing the increasing winter use in the park and will assess the environmental impacts of these proposed activities. While to some degree it is being written "after the fact," it is nevertheless a step in the right direction.

The National Forest Service is also carrying out some innovative tourism-related activities. An ambitious wilderness education program has reduced substantially the impacts of backcountry use in the popular Absaroka Beartooth Wilderness. Participants in the program learn low-impact camping techniques such as how to manage horses, use stoves (versus fuelwood), and minimize trail use/erosion.

The governor of Montana and the state Department of Fish, Wildlife and Parks recently embarked on a vision quest of their own. A State Parks Futures Committee, composed of legislators, conservationists, businessmen, and government representatives, was formed to find permanent solutions to the financial and management problems plaguing the state park system. They are preparing a report outlining the components of a well-managed system, the status of the current system, and how changes can be made. The report will include feedback from local citizens: fifteen workshops were held around the state, and local residents were invited to comment on related economic, social, and environmental issues.

The town of Dubois, Wyoming, together with the Wyoming Department of Fish and Game, the Forest Service and the Bureau of Land Management, has initiated work on an interpretive center that will focus on the natural history of the Rocky Mountain bighorn sheep, which are commonly seen by motorists passing through this scenic area. This is just one element of the "Dubois 2000" project, a community-organized effort to develop a shared vision for the future of the town. "Tourism," according to Pam Connally of the 2000 Committee, "will definitely play an important role in generating the revenue needed to make this vision a reality."

Education can often be an effective management tool for reducing visitor impacts on natural resources. It is also a prerequisite for catalyzing interest and active involvement in conservation activities. Recognizing this, a symbiotic relationship has developed between two important education-oriented facilities and the Yellowstone and Grand Teton national parks. The Teton Science School near Jackson Hole, Wyoming, and the Yellowstone Institute, located within Yellowstone Park, are nonprofit learning centers offering a wide array of field courses and hands-on natural history experiences. Both have played an important role in increasing environmental knowledge and awareness of park visitors, and certainly neither facility would exist if it were not for the spectacular open-air classrooms offered by the adjacent parks.

In August of 1990, over 100 city, county, and state planners from around the West descended on Bozeman, Montana, for the Tenth Annual Western Planners Conference. The theme focused on sustainable community development. The disadvantages and benefits of tourism, as well as how to plan for it and protect the natural resources that sustain it, were a principal focus of discussion.

Many other public and private entities are gearing up for involvement in the planning and implementation of tourism in the region. Motives for this flurry of activity range from maximizing profits to minimizing destruction. But, without doubt, linking tourism development with good planning, thorough impact assessment, a strong education orientation, identification of carrying capacity, and appropriate resource management will help to ensure local economic benefits with minimal disruption of environmental and social systems.

Conservationists have found that tourism is a double-edged sword—able to save the day if skillfully wielded, but liable to cut one's leg off if handled carelessly. In response, the Greater Yellowstone Coalition is in the process of developing a series of recommendations aimed at maximizing tourism's potential to save the day, while minimizing its destructive aspects. Though still in the formulation stage, preliminary recommendations follow.

RECOMMENDATIONS FOR LOW-IMPACT ECOTOURISM IN GREATER YELLOWSTONE

The following list of recommendations for minimizing negative tourism impacts in Greater Yellowstone is based upon the characteristics of tourism in the region, the natural and socioeconomic features affected, and the existing and projected opportunities for improving tourism management.

1. Proposed recreation and tourism activities and development should not in any way degrade Greater Yellowstone's wildland resources.
2. Environmental impact assessments should be carried out for all tourism development projects that have the potential to degrade natural and cultural resources.
3. Planning for tourism development must be well integrated with other planning efforts, particularly those related to environmental protection.
4. Visitor management should be thoroughly addressed in

the management plans for federal and state resource agencies, and in the development and master plans of cities and counties.

5. Before initiating tourism and recreational developments, the carrying capacity of the natural resources that will be impacted should be assessed. After project implementation, sites should be continually monitored, impacts identified, and measures taken to eliminate environmental degradation.

6. Tourism programs should include a strong environmental education component that provides guidelines for "low-impact tourism," stimulates an ecosystem awareness, and provides for direct participation in conservation efforts.

7. Communities developing tourism based upon natural resources should work with resource managers to ensure that the tourism resource is well protected and managed.

8. Information- and data-gathering efforts related to tourists and tourism should be improved and standardized. Trends in tourism and its impact on resource management and protection should be closely monitored.

REFERENCES

Abbey, E. 1968. *Desert Solitaire*. New York: Ballantine.

Boo, E. 1990. *Ecotourism: The Potential and Pitfalls*. Washington, D.C.: World Wildlife Fund-U.S.

Brandt, K. 1990. Assistant to the superintendent, Yellowstone National Park, personal communication.

Brock, J. et al. 1990. *Montana Tourism Marketing Research Project*. Bozeman, Montana: Montana State University.

Congressional Research Service. 1987. *Greater Yellowstone Ecosystem, An Analysis of Data Submitted by Federal and State Agencies*. Washington, D.C.: Library of Congress.

Connally, P. 1990. Member of the Dubois 2000 Committee, Dubois, Wyoming, personal communication.

D'Alesandro, N. 1985. *Concessions in Our National Parks—Are They Necessary and Appropriate?* Salt Lake City: University of Utah, College of Law.

Greater Yellowstone Coordinating Committee (GYCC). 1989. *Vision for the Future of the Greater Yellowstone Area.* Billings, Montana: GYCC.

Idaho Department of Commerce. 1989. Fremont-Teton Tourism Diversification Project. Boise: Idaho Department of Commerce.

Institute for Tourism and Recreation Research. 1989. *1988 Non-Resident Travel in Montana, An Economic Report.* Missoula, Montana: University of Montana.

Kocis, S. 1986. "The Adoption and Diffusion of Methods for Estimating Recreation Use in the Pacific Northwest Region of the U.S. Forest Service." Doctoral thesis. University of Idaho, Moscow, Idaho.

Kutay, K. 1989. "A New Ethic in Adventure Travel." *Buzzworm* 1, no. 4.

National Parks and Conservation Association (NPCA). 1988. *Parks and People: A Natural Relationship.* Washington, D.C.: NPCA.

National Park Service. 1990. *Joint Winter Use Plan for Yellowstone National Park.* Draft. Denver, Colorado: Denver Service Center.

Public Policy Center. 1985. *Building a Stronger Wyoming.* Menlo Park, California: Wyoming Futures Project, Public Policy Center.

Sax, J. 1980. *Mountains Without Handrails.* Ann Arbor, Michigan: University of Michigan Press.

Wyoming Recreation Commission. 1985. *State Comprehensive Outdoor Recreation Plan.* Cheyenne, Wyoming: State of Wyoming.

Yellowstone National Park. 1990. *Winter Use Statistics.* Yellowstone National Park.

CHAPTER 5

Ecotourism on Family Farms and Ranches in the American West

BILL BRYAN

Set at the foot of the spectacular Big Horn Mountains, the Z Bar O Ranch boasts 12,000 acres of rich bottomlands, riparian habitat, and high drylands covered with native grasses. The Tongue River runs through the property, creating natural wetlands that attract birds and large mammals from miles away.

Dick and Jean Masters, together with four generations of Masterses, live and work on the ranch, which was homesteaded by Dick's grandfather in 1884. Their primary source of income is cattle, though they grow alfalfa hay, corn, oats, barley, and soy grass, and experiment with other crops.

Several years ago, the Masterses underwent a financial crisis such that they had to find other sources of income or fold. There were several vacant guesthouses on their property, and they often had friends and family come by on visits. In reviewing alternatives, they came up with the idea of supplementing their income with a bed-and-breakfast operation.

Today, they host upwards of 100 guests during the season (May 1 to mid-October), and about 25 percent of their total income comes from visitors. They charge between $45 and $125 per night per couple, and estimate that easily half their take is profit.

Jean Masters cautions, however, that their strong earnings reflect the fact that they incurred virtually no start-up or capital costs. Guests stay in rooms that had been built for previous generations of Masterses and that had been unused. Friends in the community donated the extra household items that the Masterses needed to start out. They have hired no staff for the venture, doing everything themselves, or calling on family to help out occasionally. Their largest expenditure was producing a brochure about the ranch, and the time they spent writing letters to potential clients.

Z Bar O Ranch was the first hospitality operation in Wyoming. Today, it is one of the most successful. This is in part due to the fact that the Masterses practice sustainable agriculture and sustainable ecotourism. While much of the bottomland has been turned to irrigated farmland, the Masterses have kept the riparian habitat and wetlands untouched, in order to keep the waters of the river clean, and the wildlife abundant. They rotate their cattle to avoid placing too much pressure on the grasslands. They also rotate their crops, and use other natural alternatives before they use pesticides and chemical fertilizers. They allow hunting and fishing on their lands, but keep a strict count of what gets taken and shut their doors once the limit has been reached. Some seasons they don't allow hunting at all if they feel that there is no need for it. And they work closely with their guests, educating them about farm life, western wildlife and habitat, and the environment.

They are also well thought of in the community. They send their guests into town to sample the local restaurants and to buy souvenirs and clothes. Local schoolchildren come out to the ranch on school outings, in order to learn about how a ranch works. And the locals are not forbidden access to the Masters ranch during hunting season (which does occur at some other hospitality operations), as long as they observe certain rules of behavior and limits on game.

FARM AND RANCH HOSPITALITY: A NEW FORM OF ECOTOURISM

The Z Bar O ranch is an example of an entirely new form of ecotourism in the West that has emerged in the last five years—the ranch, or farm, hospitality business. The owners of these types of operations are real farmers and ranchers who have decided to supplement their income with money from visitors who are interested in experiencing life on a working ranch or farm, observing wildlife and wildlife habitat, and fishing and hunting on private lands. And while this chapter describes the phenomenon in the United States, it is a development that holds promise for other countries as well.

In the tri-state area of Wyoming, Montana, and Idaho, ranch and farm hospitality operations (excluding those that only offer hunting opportunities) have increased from a handful in 1985 to between seventy and ninety today. And while estimates are very rough as yet, it seems likely that they generate at least $750 million in tourist expenditures each year.

This phenomenon has its roots in the fact that the western family farm and ranch is experiencing troubled times, and that many Americans are looking for ways to "get back to the land."

The economic woes in the agricultural industry have caused many small ranchers and farmers to go out of business, liquidating their assets, and abandoning their land. Others have tried to diversify their income. Some have plunged into the ecotourism business. They are learning that there is a market for their product: people who like to spend their leisure time enjoying nature, taking advantage of photographic opportunities, learning the historical lore of the area, doing farm and ranch chores such as haying and fence mending, or just talking about the future of agriculture and other social and economic issues of the day.

The Wyoming Cooperative Extension Service has sponsored a program to actively promote farm and ranch recreation in the state. The state's Travel Commission, Health, and Economic Development departments have changed administrative procedures so that farm and ranch recreation can develop without becoming bogged down in red tape. Farm and ranch recreation enterprises in the state have set up their own trade and marketing association called the Wyoming Homestay and Outdoor Adventure Association (WHOA).

The concept has caught on in neighboring states. Colorado, Nebraska, the Dakotas, and Montana have all recognized farm/ranch recreation as a viable tourism enterprise and an excellent way to supplement farm and ranch income. Idaho is aggressively pursuing ecotourism as well, and recently sponsored a conference on farm/ranch recreation.

The Northern Rockies states—Idaho, Wyoming, and Montana—identify tourism as one of the most important sources of income for the region. The numbers of tourists are up and are continuing to rise. Ecotourists staying at farm and ranch hospitality operations represent a growing percentage of the total. Again, estimates are rough, but some put the number of annual visitors at about 3,000, and the number of visitor-days at about 11,500. This does not sound like a lot of people. And hospitality operations can net as little as $1,000 for their efforts, with the most successful seldom topping $25,000 per year. But these funds are what makes the difference for the ranch. Without this money, many family operations are sold to agribusiness, often with negative consequences for the environment. Why are people visiting these hospitality operations? The standard answer is: more people, more free time, a more mobile society, and a devalued dollar abroad.

That is part of it. But the phenomenon also has its roots in the fact that more and more people want to experience something genuine in their vacation, a "real" adventure, not a passive experience like lying on a beach. Travel specialist

Arthur Frommer, who has just published *The Future of Tourism*, writes that people want recreational experiences that challenge the mind, expand horizons, and test beliefs about their lifestyles.

Many of these people want to spend their vacations outdoors, fishing, hiking, camping, riding, bicycling, etc. They are looking for a mild climate, clear and clean air, and beautiful scenery.

Others, often first-generation urbanites, want to "return to their roots" and have a nature-oriented leisure-time experience reminiscent of the days they spent as a youth, either on the family farm or a relative's ranch or farm. Some want to meet people who have different lifestyles and make their living in ways closely related to the land.

APPROPRIATE ECOTOURISM

Ecotourism on farms and ranches can be a wonderful economic opportunity, with positive and wide-ranging social, political, and environmental benefits. However, it should not be viewed solely as an avenue for short-term financial gain.

There are a number of prerequisites to making ecotourism profitable and beneficial over the long term. First, would-be operators must decide whether offering the service is an appropriate endeavor for them, given personal traits, economic needs, state of facilities, and so forth. Second, the site must provide appropriate recreational and educational opportunities for visitors. And, third, ecotourism must be practiced in a manner appropriate to the land and overall natural environment in which the enterprise takes place.

Tourism in the Northern Rockies and other areas has sometimes been pushed in the direction of economic development for its own sake. Most published data on tourism, for example, are based on the volume of people who visit the region. Data on who spends what amount of money and for which services and commodities are known but not accorded much importance. Yet it is essential to ask which *type* of tourist should be targeted, given economic needs and the limitations of a fragile and delicate environment. Thus, planning for ecotourism in the West needs to address the impacts of the demand and what the appropriate response should be.

CHARACTERISTICS OF THE PROVIDER

The ecotourism industry is not a resource-based industrial endeavor producing a cash crop, but an economic activity in the service sector. The operator packages his or her own experiences on the farm or ranch in ways that will generate revenues. The success of this packaging is very much dependent on the personality of the provider. This must be clearly understood by the would-be provider if his or her business is to be enjoyable and successful.

In deciding whether a hospitality operation is appropriate for him or her, the potential provider should also consider whether the new economic activity will complement existing farm and ranch operations or hinder them. What might the potential conflicts be? Will the family recreation season conflict with the haying or grain harvest? Does the usual cattle roundup conflict with the hunting season? Will the sincere naïveté on the part of the urban visitor conflict with the highly opinionated farmer or rancher?

Customers probably will have certain perspectives and opinions on issues such as meat, pesticides, animals, hunting, basic farming and ranching practices, and the environment. It will be essential for providers to understand and acknowledge these perspectives.

What about the neighbors—how will they feel about the venture next door and will they be involved? What about the surrounding community—how will they view such an endeavor? Do *all* family members want to be involved in the new business?

These are the kinds of tough questions that must be asked before setting up a hospitality operation. Farm and ranch recreation should be an educational as well as a pleasurable experience. The best form of education is when both parties learn from each other. Providers must ask themselves how well they can listen to both sides of an issue, share facts versus opinions, and take constructive criticism. They must assess frankly their personalities in the area of communication and the handling of people. If strong, positive interaction with strangers is not a forte, then would-be providers should reconsider entering into the business.

QUALITY OF THE LOCATION

To be successful, a ranch or farm recreational provider must first invest time and money learning about what the nature tourist wants and expects on his or her visit, and then make sure he or she can meet those expectations.

In most cases, tourists will come from urban areas. They will require basic amenities, including clean water, electricity, heat, cleanliness, privacy, and good beds. They will expect an accessible location, but one that is sufficiently rural. The yard, lawn, and buildings must be in good repair.

They will also expect to see wildlife and beautiful scenery, as well as have the opportunity to hike, ride, and partake in other recreational activities. The location of the ranch or farm should be able to meet these expectations.

Proximity to historical sites, natural areas, or cultural attractions is also important to visitors.

APPROPRIATENESS OF LAND USE PRACTICES

Many nature tourists are likely to view ranchers and farmers as land stewards—that their land should be managed based on the underlying principle that it is being held in trust for generations to come. It is therefore particularly important for those who want to be involved in farm/ranch recreation to practice sustainable and environmentally sound agricultural activities. Farmers should carefully assess how they currently utilize the land and how those practices as well as family beliefs fit into an overall land ethic. Providers must consider issues such as the role of toxins, the concept of carrying capacity, increasing soil productivity organically, and soil conservation.

Many nature tourists see themselves as environmentalists. This is also the case for most farmers and ranchers. But, in practice, each applies their version of environmentalism differently. On the surface, there may be conflict and disagreement. As environmental issues become an even larger concern in the future, farm and ranch recreation can have enormous educational value. As never before, there is a need for people who work directly with the land to communicate with those who benefit from such efforts but are a step or two removed from the land base. Such conversations and the education that results for both parties is critical to the future of agriculture and for the future of the planet. Therefore, farm and ranch recreation is an extremely appropriate venture for the long-term health of the land resource base.

CONCLUSION

Farm and ranch recreation can provide economic, educational, and environmental benefits: however, it is not a quick economic fix and can dash just as many hopes and dreams in implementation as it creates in concept. Nevertheless, it is an exciting new trend that can contribute to the sustainable development of rural communities, and offset pressure toward less environmentally sensitive alternatives such as agribusiness.

Appendix

Farm/Ranch Hospitality Operation Checklist

In order for a farm/ranch hospitality and/or recreation operation to prosper, it is essential for entrepreneurs to approach the endeavor as a business. A great deal of work needs to be done prior to and after "hanging out a shingle" to ensure that the effort to supplement farm/ranch income will be successful.

Following is a checklist that should provide some guidance for those who are just beginning to set up a business. The list is based on field research and interviews with several farmers and ranchers currently receiving guests.

1. Assess human and physical assets.
2. Discuss realistic revenue expectations. Interview others in the business to determine how much you might expect to net.
3. Prepare a business plan. This plan should include a goal statement, expected revenues and expenses, and a marketing plan. You will need to develop a rate schedule, and determine seasons and days of operation.
4. Prepare a marketing plan and begin promoting your business to potential clients. Identify the target audience, prepare sales materials, and work to attract customers.
5. Research zoning restrictions. Although zoning should not pose a problem for rural property owners, you'll

want to be sure your property is properly zoned for farm/ranch recreations. You may need to request a variance, which can take extra time.

6. Contact key advisers. This list might include an attorney, an accountant, and state travel officials. The purpose of making these contacts is both to inform and to solicit information and advice.

7. Contact your state health administrator. Rules and regulations vis-à-vis farm/ranch recreation vary from state to state. You will need to know at the outset what is required in your state.

8. Research insurance. No industry standard exists; therefore, it is essential to "comparison shop" for reasonable insurance rates.

9. Learn tax procedures. Obtain a sales tax number (if applicable in your state), learn lodging tax requirements.

10. Register your business name with the secretary of state in your state.

11. Obtain a business license. The procedure and price vary by state and county.

12. Set house rules and develop guest procedures on the following: reservation procedures, check-in hours, checkout time, smoking policies, use of bathrooms, use of other areas in house or on ranch, fire exit plan, safety measures on the farm/ranch, use of alcohol, meal hours, pets, behavior of children.

    Guests should be informed of all pertinent policies either when a deposit request is sent out or upon arrival. A typed copy should be available in each guest room or cabin.

13. In-house policies. Just as there are rules for guests, there should also be in-house rules for family, designed to make guests comfortable and afford maximum privacy. An example might be: "Family is not allowed to use the upstairs bathroom from 7:00 A.M. to 10:00 A.M." Other issues may include mealtime manners, household duties, attitude toward and relationships with guests.

14. Prepare menus. Because food and the presentation of meals are so important to any hospitality operation, care should be taken to develop a number of wholesome, nutritious menus. Guests will not expect to be served leftovers.
15. Identify activities, recreational and otherwise, for guests. Implicit in the farm/ranch recreation business is the opportunity for guests to take part in some form of activity. It will be helpful, in this initial phase, to list every kind of activity available, from helping to can vegetables to overnight horseback trips. You can use this list to design a "guest activities calendar." Such a calendar might change weekly, monthly, and seasonally.

PART II

The Nuts and Bolts of Successful Nature Tourism

CHAPTER 6

The Economics of Nature Tourism: Determining If It Pays

PAUL B. SHERMAN AND JOHN A. DIXON

Consider a tropical rain forest somewhere in Central America. Though it is presently inaccessible, an extension of a national highway will soon open up the area. Various potential users of the resource become interested in the possibilities. A *campesino* considers the area's potential for agricultural development and sees dollar signs. A logger looks at the timber resources and also sees money to be made. A nature tourism operator reaches the same conclusion. The government, on the other hand, sees a major quandary.

Each potential user of this previously inaccessible resource seeks monetary benefits from its exploitation and use. Their different visions, however, are likely to conflict. Some uses will preclude others, though certain combinations of uses can coexist.

Governments face the difficult decision of how best to use these natural areas. Should they be preserved intact? Should they be exploited for short-term profits? Should they be converted to another use such as agriculture? Should tourism be encouraged? How should decisions be made?

Keeping the natural area relatively intact, thus ensuring the survival of the plants and animals it contains, providing opportunities for recreation and tourism, and maintaining the other benefits such as watershed protection may sound reasonable to someone who has no economic stake in the alternatives.

However, as mentioned earlier, the *campesino* or logger may also have plans for the same site. These alternative uses of natural areas often appear extremely attractive in the short term. Many tropical forests, for example, contain large amounts of valuable timber. Other areas can be converted to uses such as agriculture, grazing, or tree crops. In many cases, a traditional economic analysis would find that some form of development would provide greater financial returns than the modest direct returns from maintaining an area in its natural state, even if the latter supports ecological functions and a small-scale nature tourism industry. As a result, there is often substantial pressure to convert and exploit natural areas.

In addition to pressure on natural areas from proposed development projects, in many countries an even greater threat is gradual encroachment and resource extraction by nearby residents. These patterns of resource use, whether nonsustainable (a *campesino* clearing steep slopes for annual crop production) or sustainable (collection of various minor forest products in wooded areas), are not easily stopped by the mere creation of a protected area. The economic pressures on the resource users continue and, barring use of extreme regulatory measures, must be taken into account if effective protection is to be provided.

Thus economics, and the quest for financial returns, will most likely drive decision-making about the use of natural areas (though politics may also be a factor). The government must arbitrate and make decisions that will allow some uses and prohibit others. When deciding whether to allow the forest or other natural resources to be used for nature tourism, the government should ask the following type of economically driven questions.

1. Does nature tourism pay? That is, are the benefits from nature tourism greater than the costs?
2. Which benefits are forgone if the site is not developed for alternative uses? What are the total costs of protecting a site for nature tourism?
3. Who owns the resource? Is it publicly or privately owned?
4. What approach should be taken in carrying out an economic analysis? Should the decision-making criterion emphasize public gain or private financial benefit?
5. What are the total benefits from nature tourism, including benefits that may not be translated directly into tourist revenue dollars. Can these benefits be identified and quantified?
6. Is nature tourism an economically efficient way to generate income and help maintain and conserve natural areas?

In reality, these economic questions must be framed at two levels: financial and social. We need to know if nature tourism will pay as a business venture, and if it will pay as a social investment, particularly if governments must protect natural areas to support it.

A financial analysis of the various alternative uses of an undeveloped natural area alone is often misleading. Such an analysis is designed only to examine costs and benefits as measured by market prices—it leaves out many important factors that are not bought or sold. Many of the benefits of conserving natural areas are difficult to measure (e.g., biodiversity, watershed protection, filtering of pollutants). These benefits are not exchanged in markets and, consequently, the value of conserving, rather than developing, an area is often underestimated in a financial analysis. This leads to a bias toward development and exploitive use of an area, with the end result being that fewer natural areas are protected than would be the case if all of the benefits of conservation were acknowledged.

A social welfare analysis, on the other hand, will account for the social and intangible benefits and costs of an area, including conservation. This type of analysis can distinguish between private, financial benefits accruing to individuals or firms and public, social benefits (what economists call "social welfare benefits"). It facilitates the decision-making process by providing three categories that describe the nature and scale of the economic benefits of the site and who receives them. The three categories are: privately beneficial, socially beneficial, or undetermined benefits.

PRIVATELY BENEFICIAL

In some areas, the economic benefits directly obtainable by individuals, groups, or firms are larger than the associated costs or the benefits of alternative uses. In these cases, the individual will provide the "service" (i.e., recreation and protection of a natural area) without government intervention. Examples of such cases are not uncommon, but the areas tend to be small and the nature of the service provided rather specific.

Privately run recreational areas such as campgrounds, ski resorts, or game reserves, for example, often keep limited portions of an area in its natural state, in order to keep customers. Outstanding areas such as the Galápagos Islands or Yosemite National Park, though currently administered by national governments, are also examples of privately beneficial areas.

Some natural areas, currently unprotected, may be considered so important that private individuals or groups feel strongly enough to purchase them from their current owners. Conservation groups such as the Nature Conservancy in the United States have begun acquiring important natural areas threatened by development. These groups pool donations from their members to acquire development rights or to buy areas that might not be protected otherwise. The contributors to such private conservation efforts perceive the benefits to outweigh the costs. In addition, the sites often become nature tourism destinations for the group's members.

SOCIALLY BENEFICIAL

In this more common scenario, the net benefits to society at large are positive, but one individual or privately owned concern cannot capture all the benefits effectively and therefore is not willing to provide protection or preservation. Protection of upper watershed areas, for example, may be justified by their effects on the water supply and water quality for a downstream area, more than for their tourism receipts. In East Africa, government support of wildlife parks is usually socially beneficial in terms of attracting tourists and the wide range of associated tourist expenditures both within and outside protected areas.

Many nature tourism destinations fall in the socially beneficial category. Since these areas may not be capable of generating direct revenues greater than their costs, some government support may be needed to maintain them.

UNDETERMINED BENEFITS

In some cases, it may be difficult to determine whether the net benefits of maintaining a natural area for tourism and other uses are positive or negative. The costs of protection may be known, but the benefits may be diffuse or difficult to measure. This is especially true of wilderness areas or remote locations where nature tourism may be sporadic or of very low intensity. Governments may well decide to protect some of these areas, but at what cost and to what extent? These are issues that need to be addressed.

Let us return to our initial scenario, where the *campesino*, the logger, and the nature tourism operator are eyeing the same piece of real estate. They will assess the economic benefits and costs differently, but will use a typical financial analysis model. It is the government's responsibility to conduct a social welfare analysis that includes impacts of alternative development options, regardless of whether or not these impacts occur on-site or elsewhere in the economy.

In this chapter, we will demonstrate how to perform and implement a social welfare analysis for ecotourism projects. Our thesis is that ecotourism needs to be considered both as a business (and therefore subject to a financial profit/loss analysis) and as a type of resource use that helps ensure other, long-term social goals (such as protection of natural areas, biodiversity, or retaining options for the future).

BENEFITS AND COSTS OF NATURE TOURISM

In performing a social welfare analysis of nature tourism, we will need to weigh its costs and benefits. If the net benefits to society (total benefits minus total costs) are greater than zero, then nature tourism is a potentially desirable form of land use. However, even if these net benefits are positive, this does not imply that nature tourism is the best use; the net benefits of nature tourism must then be compared with the net benefits of other alternative forms of land use. Ideally, each piece of land should be used according to its "highest and best use," that is, the use that generates the greatest net benefits to society. In broad terms, there are three additional alternatives that should normally be considered: leaving the land in its natural state but not allowing nature tourism; developing resort tourism; or developing the land for other uses such as agriculture or housing that would normally preclude tourism.

BENEFITS

Table 6.1 shows the types of benefits that may accompany nature tourism: watershed protection, ecosystem preservation, biodiversity, education and research, consumption, nonconsumptive benefits, and future values.

While some benefits of nature tourism may be relatively easy to value (e.g., tourist receipts), others such as biodiversity, nonconsumptive benefits, and future values are more difficult to analyze (Conrad 1980). Still, much can be done

TABLE 6.1. **Benefits That Accompany Nature Tourism**

1. Watershed values
   Erosion control
   Local flood reduction
   Regulation of stream flows

2. Ecological processes
   Fixing and cycling of nutrients
   Soil formation
   Circulation and cleansing of air and water
   Global life support

3. Biodiversity
   Gene resources
   Species protection
   Ecosystem diversity
   Evolutionary processes

4. Education and research

5. Consumptive benefits
   Timber
   Wildlife products
   Nontimber forest products (e.g., edible plants, herbs, medicines, rattan, building materials, rubber)

6. Nonconsumptive benefits
   Aesthetic
   Spiritual
   Cultural/historical
   Existence value

7. Future values
   Option value
   Quasi-option value

Source: *Dixon and Sherman 1990.*

either to directly value these benefits or at least to provide a framework where choices can be made that explicitly consider qualitative benefits.

Benefits from nature tourism can be analyzed in several ways. Specific examples follow:

Spatial dimension.   Benefits can be divided into local, regional, national, or global benefits. Local benefits accrue to the immediate area. They may include employment opportunities, new markets for locally produced goods, and indirect benefits such as improved infrastructure associated with tourism development.

Regional benefits fall into the same categories, though their overall importance may be less due to the larger size of the region as compared with the local area. For example, creation of fifty jobs may be significant locally but relatively unimportant from a regional perspective.

The national benefits of tourism may include tax revenues collected from visitors, the additional foreign exchange earnings from international visitors to the country, and any capital investment from either domestic or foreign sources that might otherwise have been spent outside the country's borders. They may be larger or smaller than the local/regional benefits. If a new nature tourism development serves as a substitute for another, preexisting site within the country, there may be no additional net benefits for the nation associated with the new site. Only to the extent that the new site attracts new visitors or increases the average length of stay will the benefits associated with the new site truly add to national benefits.

The global benefits of nature tourism stem from benefits such as watershed protection, ecosystem support, biodiversity, and consumption. Since nature tourism frequently requires the preservation of an area in a relatively pristine state, other benefits associated with this protection arise. For example, nature tourism may be consistent with species and habitat protection (though not necessarily so). There may also be existence and option values generated throughout the world. One problem with these global benefits, however, is that they are freely provided—there is no obligation on the part of recipients to compensate the country of origin.

Private versus social benefits.   The broad range of benefits associated with nature tourism can be divided further into private and social benefits. The private benefits associated with nature tourism are the financial returns received by those providing tourism services. Tour operators, transportation companies, lodging operators, food and equipment suppliers—all these groups receive financial remuneration for services provided. These profits are what drive private sector interest in nature tourism.

Social benefits can be described broadly as any gains in social welfare, either direct or indirect, associated with nature tourism. Such gains may be either financial in nature or nonmonetary, such as ecological benefits. A number of the benefits listed in table 6.1, for example, are primarily social benefits: ecological processes, biodiversity, nonconsumptive benefits, and future values. Other benefits such as watershed protection and education/research are partly private, partly social benefits.

While government officials may be primarily interested in the amount of expenditures and employment opportunities generated, they also should be aware of the larger picture—that is, the social benefits associated with nature tourism. Most private sector interests will be interested only in financial aspects and specifically the profits they are able to earn. Nonprofit organizations and educational groups often fall in between—they may seek to earn at least a nominal profit but also may consider other social benefits associated with nature tourism.

Primary versus secondary benefits.   Benefits can be divided into primary and secondary tourism-related expenditures. Primary expenditures are direct purchases by tourists of goods and services. Secondary expenditures (sometimes called "indirect benefits") occur when the recipients of the primary expenditures spend the money they receive from tourists. For example, when a native tour guide is paid and then spends his salary on food and housing, these expenditures are secondary expenditures. These secondary expenditures often work their way through the system many times, creating what is termed a "multiplier effect"—the initial primary expenditures are multiplied as the money is spent and then spent again.

The extent of the multiplier effect depends on who is the recipient of the direct expenditures. If the bulk of the primary expenditures is for imported goods or services provided by foreigners, who then take the money out of the country, then little of the money is respent and the multiplier will be small. If the primary expenditures go to local entrepreneurs, who spend the money locally, and which then gets spent again locally, the multiplier will be much larger.

In each round of expenditures, the money respent is less than the amount spent in the previous round—some of the money will be saved, some will go to pay taxes, some will leave the area. The money that is not respent is known as "leakage"—it leaks out of the local economy.

The multiplier effect can also be applied to employment. The employment multiplier looks at how many jobs are indirectly created for each job directly created by the tourist operation.

COSTS

As with benefits, costs can be categorized in a number of ways and will be viewed differently from different perspectives. The following presents one potentially useful categorization of costs.

Direct costs.   Direct costs are financial outlays associated with the establishment and maintenance of a nature tourism site. These costs may be borne either by the government sector, the tour operator, or, as is often the case, split between the two. In many cases, the highest single cost is developing access to the site. By its very nature, most forms of nature tourism take place off the beaten path. While remoteness is a draw for many people, access must be easy enough not to discourage potential visitors. Depending on the site and the activity involved, access may require upgrading or development of roads, airstrips, or boat docking facilities. Since these facilities may provide benefits in addition to access to nature tourism sites, governments may be willing to contribute to their cost.

Other facilities for tourists can be developed and provided either by governments or private operators. Lodging and food service are more amenable to private development than multipurpose items such as roads. Regardless of who develops the facilities, however, it is critical that ample attention be paid to handling the wastes such as trash and sewage. The full costs of dealing with these items must be considered at the development stage. Similarly, the costs of maintaining and repairing all facilities must be accounted for.

Indirect costs. Certain types of nature tourism may be associated with damages indirectly caused by the existence of the nature tourism industry. The most common example of these indirect costs are damages caused by wildlife, either inside or beyond the boundary of the tourist enterprise. These damages may include crops trampled or eaten, as well as harm to people, livestock, or materials. Examples include damages to crops by elephants in Indonesia and Sri Lanka, predation of livestock by lions in Africa, and problems with tigers in India. These indirect costs can create local resentment of plans to expand protected areas and associated nature tourism activities.

Private operators usually will not consider these indirect costs in their financial analysis of nature tourism. Governments, on the other hand, should anticipate such problems and develop means of compensating those adversely affected. Though not compelled to compensate for such damages, governments should realize that community attitudes toward the success of nature tourism will be much more positive if nearby residents are reimbursed for any damages they suffer. The costs of such compensation programs should be considered a cost of doing business, and included in a social welfare analysis.

Opportunity costs. The opportunity costs of nature tourism are the benefits that society or individuals must give up if nature tourism precludes other uses of an area. They may include forgone resources from the area (such as timber, animals, edible plants), as well as any resources that could have been developed through more intensive exploitation or conversion to some alternative use. The magnitude of the opportunity costs will depend on the type of nature tourism and the potential alternative uses of the area. If no profitable alternative exists for the area, then the opportunity costs may be very low or even nonexistent.

Not all opportunity costs will be apparent in a standard financial analysis. Nature tourism may involve restrictions on local use of resources; for example, hunting is banned in many national parks, which means that local residents can no longer count on those resources for sustenance or livelihood. The value of products no longer available is also an opportunity cost and should be included in the analysis. As with the case of indirect costs, local residents should be compensated for any losses they suffer as a result of establishing a nature tourism site.

COMPARING COSTS AND BENEFITS

Comparing costs and benefits differs depending on whether one is using a financial or social welfare analysis. In the first case, it may try to determine the profitability of a nature tourism enterprise. Alternatively, a social welfare analysis may seek to determine whether nature tourism is socially desirable. The latter is much broader in scope, and often more difficult. While there are well-established methods of financial analysis based on market prices, social welfare analysis must consider a broader range of benefits than just financial returns. All effects on individuals—whether monetary, environmental, cultural, or otherwise—must be included. Since many of these effects have no market prices, the task of placing values on them is a complex one, too complex to develop here. Interested readers can find details on valuing environmental effects in Dixon et al. (1988), Hufschmidt et al. (1983), or Dixon and Sherman (1990).

Financial analysis. A private operator considering development of a nature tourism site or coordinating trips to an established site should perform a financial analysis to determine the profitability of the proposed investment. The financial analysis begins with a list of the expected costs and benefits that will occur in each year. Capital costs can be entered in the year they are spent, spread over the life of the project (amortized) if internal funds are used, or spread over the loan period if costs are to be financed through debt. In addition to the initial capital costs, annual operating and maintenance costs are included, along with expected changes over time. The interest rate used will be either the market rate of interest (if funds are borrowed) or if internal funds are used, the opportunity cost of capital (the returns that these funds could generate if invested in another project). Revenues will be based on projections of number of visitors multiplied by the revenue per visitor.

Governments may also choose to perform a financial analysis when considering nature tourism as a form of land use. This will show whether nature tourism will pay for itself, or whether a subsidy will be needed. In some situations, subsidies may be warranted—if, for example, nature tourism will achieve other national goals, such as increasing foreign exchange receipts or developing employment opportunities in low-income regions.

Social welfare analysis. From a national perspective, the economic analysis should consider the social benefits, and social costs, of the proposed activity. The most common form of social welfare analysis is benefit-cost analysis (BCA). Like financial analysis, BCA involves the evaluation of a stream of benefits and costs over some chosen period of time. Here, however, the focus is not just on financial costs and benefits but on the social welfare of the community as well. The prices used are not always market prices; instead, what might be called "economic efficiency prices" are used. Distortions such as those caused by taxes, subsidies, or regulatory effects are removed so that prices reflect true resource commitments to society.

BCA may also include effects that are ignored in a financial analysis. If tourism is accompanied by some undesirable environmental effects, the value of these effects is also considered. This is true whether these effects occur at the tourism site or some distance away from it.

Overall, there are a number of differences between a social BCA (sometimes referred to as a SBCA) and a financial analysis (see table 6.2). Whereas a financial analysis includes subsidies, taxes, and interest payments, an SBCA considers these as transfer payments. A transfer payment is simply a transfer of resources between two different units within the economy; for example, income tax is a transfer from an individual to the government. Transfer payments change the distribution of income but do not change the overall amount of income. Hence, a BCA does not include them in evaluating overall social welfare changes.

A financial analysis usually uses market borrowing rates to determine the discount rate; a SBCA uses a social discount rate that is usually lower and reflects a number of societal decisions. Prices may be similarly adjusted. Details of the differences between financial and SBCA can be found in Hufschmidt et al. (1983) and Dixon and Hufschmidt (1986). These references also discuss decision criteria such as net present value (NPV), internal rate of return (IRR), and benefit-cost ratio (BCR).

While relatively straightforward in theory, preparing a BCA for a proposed nature tourism project is often difficult in practice. Evaluating the environmental and cultural effects, both positive and negative, associated with nature tourism is particularly problematic. In most cases, at least a portion of these effects will remain unquantified. Therefore, the quantified net benefits will often be less than the actual total benefits from nature tourism.

If the quantifiable benefits alone are greater than the measured costs (and also greater than the net benefits from alternative uses of the site), nature tourism is a viable option. When the quantifiable benefits associated with tourism are less than the costs, however, or when the net benefits are positive but less than the benefits associated with another alternative use, the decision-making process becomes more difficult. In both these cases, governments must decide whether the nonquantified benefits associated with nature

**TABLE 6.2   A Comparison of Financial and
Social Benefit-Cost Analysis**

	Financial	*SBCA*
Focus	Net returns to equity capital or to private group or individual	Net returns to society
Purpose	Indication of incentive to adopt or implement	Determine if government investment is justified on economic efficiency basis
Prices	Market or administered (may assume that markets are perfect or that administered prices have compensated for imperfections)	May require "shadow prices" (e.g., adjustments for monopoly in markets, external effects, unemployed or underemployed factors, overvalued currency)
Taxes	Cost of production	Transfer payments to governments—deducted from costs of project inputs and outputs
Subsidies	Source of revenue	Transfer payments from governments—value of subsidies added to project costs of inputs and outputs
Loans	Increase capital resources available	A transfer payment; transfer a claim to resource flow
Interest or loan repayment	A financial cost; decreases capital resources available	A transfer payment
Discount rate	Marginal cost of money; market borrowing rate	Opportunity cost of capital; social time preference rate
Income distribution	Can be measured by net returns to individual factors of production such as land, labor, and capital	Is not considered in standard economic efficiency analysis; can be done as separate analysis or as weighted efficiency analysis

SOURCE: *Dixon, James and Sherman 1989; adapted from Hitzhusen 1982.*

tourism justify either a subsidy or forgoing the additional benefits associated with the alternative land uses.

The siting of major infrastructure facilities, such as dams, ports, or airports, may have potential direct or indirect impacts on areas used for or suitable for nature tourism. The social BCA of such projects must examine all the impacts as well as other possible alternatives. (The suggested project is assumed to pass a financial analysis—e.g., positive net benefits—or else it would not have been proposed.)

A classic case in the United States occurred in Hell's Canyon (Krutilla and Fisher 1985). In this case, a series of dams would have flooded Hell's Canyon and disrupted the last wild river in the area, a popular recreation site for residents and visitors. In an innovative study, Krutilla and Fisher examined a number of aspects of the preservation-versus-development alternatives. In the end, the dams were not built and the canyon was left intact. This type of analysis is sometimes referred to as "opportunity cost analysis." Here, the analyst compares the net economic benefits of alternative uses. While the net economic benefits of development usually can be monetized relatively precisely (in the case of Hell's Canyon, these were power generation benefits), nature tourism and the associated ecological protection often involve many nonquantifiable benefits. The net monetary benefits of development are first compared with the quantifiable benefits from nature tourism. If the former are larger than the latter, then the analyst looks at how large the nonquantifiable benefits would have to be to outweigh the total benefits of development. If it appears that the nonquantified benefits will be at least this large, then nature tourism would be the preferred option.

In addition to environmental and cultural effects, other nonquantifiable effects include job creation and foreign exchange impacts. While these may be desirable, they are not easily converted to dollar terms. Moreover, these effects must be compared with other possibilities for the area—while creation of twenty jobs in a nature tourism enterprise might seem beneficial, it is not truly so if some alternative development would provide forty jobs. As discussed earlier, the benefits of nature tourism must be weighed against the best alternative use—only the difference between the two alternatives is actually a benefit.

In some cases, a natural area may have been given protected status already, and the analysis is being performed only to determine whether or not nature tourism should be allowed. In this case, the analysis is simpler, since development alternatives need not be evaluated. First, the financial costs and benefits of nature tourism are estimated. The net financial benefits are then compared with other effects, such as environmental impacts (which should also be monetized to the extent possible). All of this information is then used to determine if social welfare will be improved by allowing tourism.

DISTRIBUTION OF BENEFITS AND COSTS

The potential profitability of a nature tourism enterprise is only one of many factors used to determine whether or not it is desirable. While profitability may be the most important factor in a private operator's decision, governments may be more interested in how the benefits and costs will be distributed. If nature tourism will provide large profits to a foreign-owned company but adversely affect local residents, it may not be in the country's best interests to allow it. On the other hand, a locally owned company that makes an effort to include nearby residents may be much more desirable, even if the enterprise generates little or no profit.

Consider a publicly owned site suitable for outdoor recreation and believed to be capable of supporting a profitable tourism operation. Three alternatives exist: selling the site to a private operator; leasing the use of the site to a private operator; or establishing a government-owned and -operated enterprise.

If the government sells the site, it loses a great deal of control over what type of development and management occurs. The buyer will probably attempt to maximize profits, possibly at the expense of social benefits. On the other hand, if the government leases the rights to use the site, it can establish conditions under which the leaseholder must operate. Under this setup, the government can mandate conditions that are more socially beneficial by, for example, establishing a minimum percentage of jobs that must go to local residents or limiting the allowable number of visitors per year.

Governments can also choose to operate the tourism enterprise alone. While governments often may be less efficient than the private sector, this option gives the government the greatest leeway in operating the tourism enterprise in a manner that maximizes local benefits. Such a policy may, however, be at the expense of profits. Governments must make a policy decision on this issue—does the increase in local benefits outweigh the reduction in profits?

Private ownership of nature tourism sites may be a viable option in some cases. While governments may have less oversight authority, a private owner will recognize that it is in his own self-interest to maintain the site to ensure its continued attraction to visitors. Monteverde Reserve in Costa Rica and the Community Baboon Sanctuary in Belize are but two examples of successful privately owned nature tourism destinations (Boo 1990).

Ideally, nature tourism should be beneficial for everyone involved—tourism operators receive profits, governments receive tax revenues and foreign exchange, visitors enjoy their experience, and local residents receive jobs and increased income from visitor expenditures. Too often, however, this is not the case for the latter. Unlike everyone else whose participation is voluntary, local residents may be unwilling participants and are the ones who lose.

Opening an area to tourism often means a dramatic change in lifestyle for local residents. Depending on their previous level of isolation, village life may be totally disrupted by drastic cultural changes. The introduction of relatively wealthy visitors may cause large price increases and shortages of certain goods in local markets. While this may mean profits for a few, the general population often suffers ill effects. In some cases, markets in drugs and prostitution, and adoption of other undesirable practices, may develop.

Such negative impacts need not always occur, however. With proper foresight, many can be avoided or minimized. Given the importance of this issue, special attention must be given to ways of maximizing local benefits; this topic is discussed more fully in the next section.

In addition to the effects on local people, the effects on the local environment must also be considered. These can arise either directly, as a result of tourism and the additional people using the area, or indirectly, from increased access associated with tourism development. Erosion from hiking trails, deforestation for firewood, increased trash and sewage, clearing for accommodation facilities—these consequences and others can be severe in the absence of adequate regulatory and enforcement efforts by the authority responsible. And if a new road is built to ease access for tourists, for example, it also may make it easier for people to move into the area, with subsequent clearing of forests for farmland. Governments should take measures to ensure that this secondary development does not unduly threaten the area.

The adverse effects of these impacts are often felt hardest at the local level. If tourism is not to "destroy" itself, proper planning and management are critical at an early stage.

Nature tourism can also bring about positive influences on the environment. Revenues collected through entrance fees, hotel taxes, sales tax, or other means can provide much needed funds for natural area protection and management. Properly allocated, these funds can be used to improve an area and minimize any negative environmental effects associated with tourism.

The distribution of benefits and costs can be considered within an economic analysis in two ways. The analysis could include only those benefits and costs that remain in the country (or region or village). This would eliminate operations that primarily benefit outside interests at the expense of local residents. Alternatively, weights can be placed on benefits and costs that accrue to different groups. For example, benefits that accrue to local residents in poor villages might be multiplied by a factor of two, while benefits to wealthy developers might be weighted by only a fraction. Similarly, costs that adversely affect local residents might be given greater weight than those affecting the wealthy. (Use of weights in BCA is discussed extensively in sources such as Ray 1984 and Squire and van der Tak 1975).

It is also possible to set a constraint on the allowable distribution of benefits. This involves setting targets that establish a minimum acceptable distribution of benefits among a designated low-income group or area. Only projects that will provide a certain percentage of benefits to members of this group are given consideration under this scenario.

NATURE TOURISM AND ECONOMIC DEVELOPMENT

Properly implemented, nature tourism can integrate conservation and rural development by helping to protect valuable natural areas by providing revenues for planning and management, stimulating economic development through tourism expenditures, and providing jobs and markets for local goods.

Nature tourism has the potential to help economic development at both the local and the national level. Depending on the scale of the nature tourism industry relative to the size of the local economy, the effect on the local level can be anywhere from minimal to substantial. At the national level, nature tourism is likely to have less impact, but it still may have significant influence in countries with small economies or where the potential size of the industry is very large. In Kenya, for example, the safari industry generates foreign exchange earnings of some $350 million to $400 million per year and is Kenya's largest source of foreign exchange.

In this section, we will first look at how national and local governments can maximize the revenues they receive from nature tourism. Then we will discuss how to maximize benefits for local residents.

MAXIMIZING GOVERNMENT REVENUES

While nature tourism has the potential to provide substantial benefits to countries with outstanding nature tourism sites, this will not always be the case. Too often the majority of benefits accrue to the tour operator and little remains in-country. Boo (1990) cites a World Bank study (Frueh 1988) that estimates that over one-half of gross tourism revenues in the developing countries leak back to developed countries. This is hypothesized to be even higher in the least-developed countries, where most of the goods used by tourists are imported (Mathieson and Wall 1982). Nevertheless, there are a number of mechanisms governments can put in place to increase the benefits their country receives from nature tourism.

User fees. The easiest method of capturing benefits from nature tourism is to charge a fee to use the area. Though many countries already charge small fees at cultural sites and in national parks, few countries have instituted fee schedules that reflect consumers' willingness to pay. While a small, token payment is clearly better than no fee at all, there is no reason for a country, especially a developing country, to subsidize the cost of foreigners' visits.

Developing countries should consider adopting a two-tier fee system, with a lower charge for domestic residents and a higher charge for international visitors. Some countries have already instituted such a system; China, for example, uses a two-tiered fee structure for most cultural and historic sites. Given the expense of international travel, even a relatively high fee of US $10 or more per day would probably have a negligible effect on the total number of visitors. This is especially true for unique areas that can handle only a limited number of visitors. In the Mountain Gorilla Project (MGP) in Rwanda, for example, foreigners are charged an entrance fee of $170 per day and yet demand has remained strong. It has been noted that this is among the highest such fee charged anywhere in the world and may be near the upper limit of visitor willingness-to-pay (Lindberg 1989).

Figure 6.1   *Mountain gorilla in Rwanda.*

PHOTO: Craig Sholley, Courtesy of International Expeditions, Inc.

User fees help to support the Saba Marine Park in the Netherland Antilles. Since the main attraction of the park is its scuba diving and snorkeling, divers are charged $1 per dive, paid through the dive boat operators, to support conservation activities. This modest fee provides valuable revenue and is unnoticed in the overall costs of diving (van't Hof 1989).

Fees for government-owned accommodations near nature tourism sites should be priced at levels comparable to privately owned accommodations. Camping fees could also be set on a two-tier system as suggested for entrance fees. At present, many national parks charge very low accommodation or camping fees, resulting in excess demand for these facilities and insufficient funds for operation and maintenance. Businesslike behavior can be as beneficial to public operations as it is to private ones.

Concession fees.   In addition to charging fees directly to visitors, fees can also be charged to individuals or firms who provide services to these visitors. This would include licensing of concessions for food, lodging, transportation, guide services, and retail stores. By auctioning or leasing the rights to operate such concessions, governments can control the types of development in and nearby nature tourism sites and simultaneously raise revenues to help maintain the area. Governments also can impose conditions on concession leases to address other objectives such as hiring local employees or selling locally produced goods.

Royalties.   Establishment of royalty systems on activities and products in tourist areas is another potential source of revenue. For example, permission for books, photos, or films to be made at tourism sites could be exchanged for some percentage of the revenues made on these items. In the Saba Marine Park, sales of T-shirts and guidebooks are a major source of revenue. Such souvenir sales, either direct or via licensing, can be major revenue producers.

Tax policies.   Governments can enact tax policies to increase the revenues they receive from nature tourism. Perhaps the most common type of tax is a hotel room tax, which is also relatively popular among residents since it falls primarily on visitors. Hotel room taxes of 5 to 10 percent are found in many areas.

Special taxes also can be enacted near popular tourist sites. In prewar Cambodia, for example, the famous complex of ruins associated with Angkor Wat was maintained by the government but was completely open to visitors without any formal payment. This enhanced the visitors' enjoyment of the site and allowed casual exploration. The government, however, collected a special tax on all hotel rooms in the nearby town of Siemréap to support its conservation and preservation efforts. Since virtually all visitors to Angkor stayed in these hotels (and the ruins were the main reason for people coming to the town), this was an effective and unobtrusive means of revenue collection.

Other forms of taxes include sales or excise taxes on

tourist-related goods and services. These might be levied on food bought in restaurants, specialized equipment, and tour guide services.

Donation programs. Governments can take advantage of the increasing international awareness of the problems faced by important natural areas by establishing and promoting donation programs. Such programs can be geared toward both tourists and nontourists. For tourists, guides can point out the problems of protecting the area, and encourage donations to help alleviate these pressures. To reach nontourists (and potential tourists), governments might join with conservation groups in a campaign to raise funds from interested individuals.

MAXIMIZING LOCAL BENEFITS

One of the critical issues concerning nature tourism is its impact on local residents, and especially rural villagers, in developing countries. Since much of the growth in nature tourism will take place in such areas, it is important that steps are taken at an early stage to ensure that local residents benefit from the tourist industry.

The most direct way of benefiting local communities is to employ as many residents as possible in tourism-related services. This includes jobs in restaurants, accommodation facilities, and as guides. Other employment possibilities include construction activities, helping to build trails, providing daily maintenance, and retail sales. If local workers do not possess the skills needed, training programs should be considered before bringing in workers from other areas.

Use of locally produced goods will also benefit the community. Governments and/or NGOs can help farmers grow crops and livestock to supply tourist facilities. Promotion of local handicrafts also provides income-earning opportunities.

Local residents also will benefit if a portion of fees collected from nature tourism is earmarked for them. This is especially important if local residents have had to give up use of an area to ensure its continued existence for tourism. For example, in many countries, collection of firewood, food, timber, or other products is not allowed in national parks. This loss of income may be devastating to people already living at or near subsistence levels.

Using a portion of the fees collected to compensate local residents provides a means of offsetting these losses. In the Chitwan National Park in Nepal, for example, conservation of this important rhino habitat is promoted by allowing villagers to harvest elephant grass periodically, thereby helping to meet their needs for income from this valuable thatch material while discouraging illegal harvest of park resources (MacKinnon et al. 1986).

Compensation can be provided in a number of ways. One possibility is to develop alternative supplies of the resource outside the tourist destination. Woodlots for firewood, captive breeding for wildlife, and farms or plantations for plant species are examples.

Developing a substitute for the lost resource is another form of compensation. If the resource was used for food, for example, a different food crop could be substituted. If it was used to generate income, other types of income-generating activities can be used to offset losses to local residents.

Fees collected from nature tourism also can be used for community development activities. Construction of schools, sanitation facilities, electricity, water systems, and health clinics are potential forms of compensation. Residents must be made aware, however, that the provision of these facilities are, at least in part, compensation for losses associated with tourism.

Compensation is also warranted in cases where there are indirect costs to local residents from nature tourism, for example, damage from wildlife. One example of compensation is the case of traditional Masai herders and Kenya's Amboseli National Park. Both the Masai cattle and the area's wildlife depend on water and pasturelands located within and outside the park; the needs and range of both cattle and wildlife change during the year depending on the amount of rainfall and pasture availability. Restricting wildlife to the park's boundaries and excluding all cattle would result in a decreased population of both.

A compromise solution between the local Masai and the park authorities resulted in substantial economic gains to both parties. The solution included payment of a grazing compensation to the Masai to cover their livestock losses to wildlife migrants. According to Western (1984), the net monetary gain to the park from use of Masai lands is about $500,000 per year and the benefits from the park to the Masai result in an income 85 percent greater than from cattle herding alone. (There remain, however, significant conflicts between the park and the Masai; see chapter 2.)

Schemes such as those described in this section are vital if nature tourism is to benefit, rather than hurt, local communities. They also help to discourage activities that may damage tourism by providing alternatives. An International Union for the Conservation of Nature (IUCN) report discusses a number of such schemes that have been successful at both benefiting local communities and protecting natural resources (McNeely 1988).

EXAMPLES OF ECONOMIC ANALYSES OF NATURE TOURISM

KHAO YAI NATIONAL PARK, THAILAND

Khao Yai, Thailand's first national park, is located about 160 kilometers northeast of Bangkok (see figure 6.2). Covering 2,168 square kilometers, Khao Yai has been one of Thailand's most popular parks since its establishment in 1962 and is one of ten ASEAN Heritage Parks and Reserves (NPD 1986).

Khao Yai provides a number of benefits both to the surrounding region and to the nation. It is a premier tourist

Figure 6.2   *Khao Yai National Park, Thailand.*

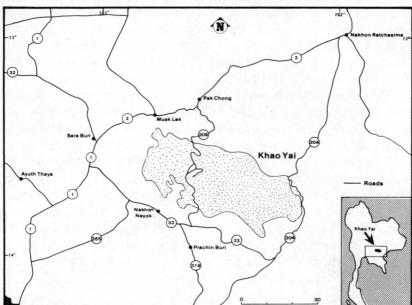

Source: *Dixon and Sherman 1990.*

destination in the region, with between 250,000 and 400,000 visits per year. Since it contains most of the remaining forest in the area, it is of critical importance for wildlife and also profoundly affects the hydrology of the region. Four river basins have their headwaters in Khao Yai, and two major reservoirs are dependent on water from the park.

In addition to being the oldest national park in Thailand, Khao Yai is also one of the most popular and well-developed parks for recreation. Located approximately three hours away from Bangkok by car, Khao Yai attracts large numbers of both Thais and foreigners. Visits to Khao Yai more than tripled between 1977 and 1987.

A recent survey of Khao Yai visitors designed by the authors and members of the World Wide Fund for Nature Beneficial Use Project, and undertaken by the latter group

between March and May 1988, found that the site was visited mainly as a nature tourism destination. For foreigners
visiting the park, more than 62 percent stated that wildlife
viewing was one of their three main reasons for coming to
Khao Yai. This was followed by scenery (58 percent), relaxation (43 percent), and hiking (41 percent).

Thai nationals overwhelmingly said that enjoying the scenery (54 percent) was their main reason for visiting Khao
Yai. (Note that relaxation was not given as a separate choice
in the Thai-language version of the survey, so percentages
are not directly comparable.) Adding the percentage of
people indicating any specific activity as one of their top
three reasons for coming to Khao Yai showed that viewing
scenery was still number one (86 percent), followed by
seeing the waterfalls (58 percent), wildlife viewing (36 percent), picnicking (29 percent), and overnight camping (25
percent). (More detailed responses from this survey can be
found in Dobias et al. 1988).

Financial benefits.   Both the National Parks Division (NPD)
and Tourist Authority of Thailand (TAT) operate lodging
facilities in Khao Yai. Revenues from NPD-operated accommodations were almost 1.5 million baht in 1987 (approximately 26 baht equals US $1). Dobias et al. (1988) report
that the TAT income from lodging in 1987 was almost 5 million baht, while TAT-run restaurants received 4.2 million
baht in income. TAT also received 400,000 baht from golf
course fees, 318,000 baht from their souvenir shop, and
230,000 baht from nighttime excursions to view wildlife
with spotlights. Thus, TAT's gross income was more than 10
million baht in 1987, while its expenditures during that year
were approximately 3.3 million baht. While these figures do
not include prior capital expenditures to build facilities, it
is nonetheless clear that TAT's operations are profitable. Unfortunately, all profits from TAT's operations go to TAT and
not to the NPD and, therefore, they do not contribute to the
management and preservation of the park.

Gate fees from admission to the park in recent years
ranged from 1.6 to 2.4 million baht per year. Adding the gate

fees and NPD-operated accommodation charges, tourism directly contributed approximately 3 million baht in 1987. In addition, NPD received 150,000 baht in concession fees from the four restaurants/food stalls within park boundaries.

The Beneficial Use Project (Dobias 1988; Dobias et al. 1988) has generated some interesting data on the expenditures of both Thai and foreign visitors to the park. In general, foreign visitors spend more per person than do Thai visitors. Based on data from organized bus tours, average daily per person expenses for foreign visitors range from 500 to 800 baht, of which the formal admission fee is less than 1 percent. Clearly, gate receipts are only a very small fraction of people's willingness-to-pay to visit Khao Yai.

With more than 400,000 visitors per year, the total expenditures generated by Khao Yai tourism are large—from 40 million to 200 million baht ($1.5 to $7.7 million) if per capita expenditures are 100 to 500 baht. These expenditures, of course, are not an economic measure of the value of the park. To determine the true economic (i.e., social welfare) gain from visiting Khao Yai, we would need to measure consumer's surplus, that is, the maximum willingness-to-pay over and above the actual cash costs of visiting Khao Yai. This amount could be estimated by carrying out a travel-cost study, an approach widely used to value the nonpriced benefits enjoyed by visitors to parks and other recreational areas. By carefully controlling for origin, visitor background, and other variables, the pattern of recreational use of a park provides the data from which a demand curve and, in turn, consumer's surplus can be estimated (see Hufschmidt et al. 1983 for a more detailed description).

In sum, the financial contribution of tourism is already substantial and can be expected to increase in the future. Bangkok is near Khao Yai and as incomes rise and fewer alternative open areas remain, Khao Yai will become increasingly valuable. Foreign tourism could also increase with improved facilities and promotion. Furthermore, virtually all Khao Yai tourism activities are restricted to a very small part of the park accessible from the one north-south road. More than 90 percent of the park is completely undeveloped and inaccessible, other than on foot. Future expansion of facilities is likely. VALUE: Tourism-related expenditures are 100 to 200 million baht (roughly US $4 to $8 million) per year, and estimates of consumer's surplus (an economic measure) are from 10 to 25 million baht per year.

Biodiversity/ecological benefits.   Maintaining Khao Yai as a national park for nature tourism and other uses provides benefits by protecting biological diversity and maintaining ecological processes. Khao Yai's rich diversity of plants and animals makes it an important reserve for many species. Although most famous for its elephants, numerous other species contribute to its biological diversity. In addition to the pure "existence value" of species diversity, it also provides a powerful pull for tourists. We are not able, however, to place a monetary value on many aspects of the current and future values of the benefits of maintaining biodiversity. VALUE: Undetermined. Expenditures on research and education related to species in Khao Yai total 1 to 2 million baht per year. Option/existence value based on Khao Yai's role as an elephant sanctuary is estimated at more than 120 million baht per year (see Dixon and Sherman 1990 for more information on how this figure was determined).

Watershed protection.   Khao Yai provides important watershed benefits in terms of the quantity, quality, and timing of water flows. The reservoirs located downstream depend on Khao Yai's watershed protection function. Maintaining Khao Yai in its current state for nature tourism and other uses will preserve these benefits as well. VALUE: Can be calculated but undetermined at present.

Management costs.   The present annual management budget for Khao Yai is about 3.4 million baht. Implementation of the Khao Yai Management Plan (NPD 1986) to meet protection, interpretation, and development goals will result in increased annual budgets and large capital expenditures in the next few years. With its large area and closely settled borders, greater effort is needed to support programs that help improve the standard of living of nearby residents, thereby reducing their dependence on illegal and unsustainable uses of the park. cost: Current government management costs are 3 to 4 million baht per year but will rise significantly over the next few years.

Opportunity costs.   A variety of development benefits are lost because of protection. Foremost are water resource development, timber harvesting, and agriculture. The potential economic benefits from agriculture appear to be relatively small and high extraction costs for timber limit its profitability. Precise estimates of these opportunity costs require more data. Impacts on tourism, biodiversity, and ecological processes, if these activities were allowed, may be large.

Another major category of opportunity costs is the loss of income to local villagers due to prohibitions on the gathering and harvesting of plants and animals in the park. Note that the two categories are not cumulative since development of park resources would also result in a loss of opportunity to collect plants and animals. value: A rough "guesstimate" of the reduction in villager-derived income from park resources is 27 million baht per year, though this amount would probably not be sustainable and would result in significant damage to highly valued species (Dixon and Sherman 1990).

Overall, Khao Yai is a good example of a protected area that fits the socially beneficial category. It provides recreational, wildlife habitat, and watershed benefits that are quantifiable in physical, and in some cases economic, terms. It also provides less tangible benefits in terms of preservation of forest cover and associated biological diversity. Without government intervention, however, such a large area could not exist. The benefits are too diffuse and the financial returns from preservation would be outweighed by the direct benefits from exploitation of Khao Yai's timber, land, and animal resources.

Management issues.   Many areas just inside the park are heavily degraded. These areas should be made into buffer zones and managed to provide benefits to nearby villagers.

Programs should be developed in these areas to promote production of plants that are currently being poached within the park or to establish other opportunities to supplement villager incomes. These programs could be paid for, at least partially, with a percentage of tourism revenues. Once established, penalties for poaching beyond the buffer zone should be strictly enforced. However, limited hunting of certain species could be allowed in the buffer zones. Such a policy would have to be accompanied by a clear demarcation of park boundaries.

Certain tourist development activities could also have secondary benefits. Development of organized multiday hikes could provide employment opportunities for local villagers as guides and support staff. One program of this type has already begun at Ban Sap Tai village under the auspices of a WWF project (Dobias et al. 1988). These hikes could also be accompanied by guards who would help patrol forest areas currently not guarded effectively.

In 1987, fees from concessions, accommodations, and entrance were almost equal to the budget allocated to Khao Yai (3.18 million baht versus 3.38 million baht respectively). If the NPD were allowed to take over facilities currently run by the Tourist Authority of Thailand (TAT), it is likely that Khao Yai could more than pay for itself with direct revenues from tourism.

The NPD should also consider establishing a two-tier fee system. Current entrance fees, though reasonable for Thais, are extremely low by foreign standards. Fees probably could be raised to ten times their current levels without significantly reducing the number of foreign visitors.

WILDLIFE PARKS IN EAST AFRICA

The wildlife parks of East Africa, particularly in Kenya and Tanzania, are extremely popular nature tourism destinations. Although both countries have spectacular scenery featuring mountains (Kilimanjaro, Mount Kenya), the Great Rift Valley, and a tropical coast, it is the game parks that attract visitors from around the world.

Nature tourism in Kenya is big business—worth an estimated $350 to $400 million per year. It also provides a substantial indirect demand for goods and services produced by the local economy and job opportunities for local residents. In addition, the foreign exchange brought in by visitors is important to the national economy. While these benefits are necessarily strict financial benefits (large amounts do not accrue to individuals), they are important social benefits. As a result, these game parks can be considered to fit in the "socially beneficial" category.

Wildlife parks require large amounts of area but often occupy land that is semiarid and has only limited alternative uses—usually grazing of livestock. A number of studies have compared the benefits from protection and its associated tourism with extensive agricultural use (grazing or crops). In one study, the estimated tourism value of protecting an area to maintain a big-animal population (e.g., lions, elephants) was over $40 per hectare versus $0.80 per hectare under "optimistic" agricultural returns from livestock grazing (Western and Thresher 1973). Even if these numbers are somewhat questionable from a technical economic viewpoint, it is clear that many areas yield much more revenue when managed for protection and nature tourism than they would under marginal agricultural development.

Western and Henry (1979) estimated the gross worth of lions in Amboseli National Park in Kenya, in terms of generating tourism revenues, to be $27,000 each per year; an elephant herd was estimated to be worth $610,000 per year. These are social returns from tourism. Yet a poacher is not interested in the larger social benefits and will kill an animal to earn a few hundred dollars.

Thresher (1981) also considered the economics of lions in Amboseli National Park in Kenya. Based on survey results, it was determined that the average visitor to Amboseli spent seventy minutes looking for and then viewing lions, or 30 percent of the average four hours spent on wildlife viewing per visit. Through a series of assumptions about Amboseli's lion population, the number of adult-maned lions, and average success rate in viewing one, Thresher determined that an individual lion will draw $515,000 in foreign exchange receipts over a fifteen-year period (with a 10 percent discount rate). This social measure of the value of a lion as a tourist attraction can be compared with the private returns of a lion as a hunting resource: a twenty-one-day lion hunt will cost a nonresident hunter about $8,500. The lowest value for a lion is the retail price for a well-cured skin: somewhere between $960 and $1,325.

This example illustrates one approach to estimating the varying direct values (both economic and financial) of the lion as a natural resource. Tourism is clearly the most efficient use of the lion—it generates a very large amount of foreign exchange over time and does not require the death of the animal. The lion is much less valuable as quarry or as a cured skin (in many cases, the two are added: lion hunts often result in lion skins).

The parallels with elephants are very close—they are much more valuable as a tourism attraction than for their ivory. Yet in the past decade, Africa's elephant population has decreased by 50 percent from 1.2 million to just over 600,000 (Mastri 1989). Kenya and Tanzania, both major nature tourism destinations, have suffered major losses to poachers—since 1981, Kenya has lost two-thirds of its elephant population, with fewer than 20,000 remaining. The recent ban on all international trade in elephant products (including ivory) and enhanced antipoaching measures appear to be having some positive effect.

In a 1989 study, Brown and Henry surveyed tourists and tour operators in Kenya to estimate the monetary value assignable to elephant viewing within the safari industry. Using two different approaches, they estimated that elephants contributed a consumer's surplus (an economic measure) of from $25 to $30 million annually. This was about 13 percent of the total consumer's surplus of $182 to $218 million of the 300,000 or so adults who went on safari.

The social benefits of nature tourism in these areas are large. However, actions by individuals, either poachers or farmers/pastoralists who are using the park's resources for personal gain, threaten to destroy the nature tourism industry. A remote semiarid landscape without animals will have little appeal in the international nature tourism market.

A major management challenge, therefore, is to find ways to include the individuals who live adjacent to the parks in the economic benefits generated by tourism. The Amboseli/ Masai case cited earlier in this chapter is one example. Community involvement and support for development are essential if the resource degradation presently found in many game parks is to be reduced.

Controlling poachers may be a bigger challenge. Animal poachers frequently come from some distance outside the area and are difficult to regulate. Efforts are needed both on the demand side (reducing worldwide demand for and trade in poached products, thereby reducing their value) and on the supply side (controlled harvesting of desired products on a sustainable basis). In many cases, regulation and police enforcement are also needed to control the killing of these animals.

NATURE TOURISM IN THE CARIBBEAN

Tourism is the largest single industry in the Caribbean. Some countries are almost entirely dependent on tourism revenues while others have more mixed economies. One small but rapidly growing segment of the tourism industry is nature tourism.

Nature tourism is receiving increased attention now as a result of two important trends. One is the growing demand for "off-the-beaten-track" destinations within the international tourism industry. The second trend is the new emphasis by park managers on increasing support (both political and financial) for protected area management through integrating economic components into conservation activities. As economic growth and development proceed, the number of "wild places" will decrease and their attractiveness will increase. As part of a mixed bundle of attractions, nature tourism can play an increasingly useful role as various countries seek to differentiate their "product" in the world market.

Figure 6.3.   *Saba Marine Park, Netherlands Antilles.*

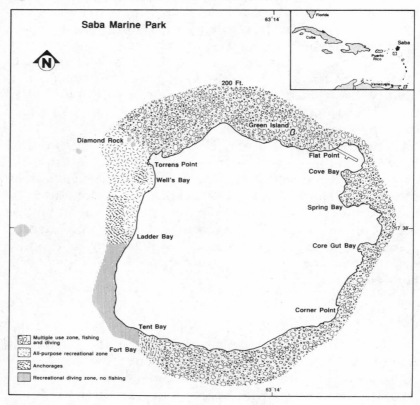

SOURCE: *Saba Conservation Foundation.*

The small island of Saba, part of the Netherland Antilles, is a well-known nature tourism destination. Located in the Leeward Islands of the Lesser Antilles (see figure 6.3), Saba is a high volcanic island, with a population of some 1,200 people on its twelve and a half square kilometers.

The Saba Marine Park, established in June 1987, includes the entire coastal environment. The primary emphasis is marine tourism, in particular scuba diving and snorkeling (van't Hof 1989). The park has used an innovative combination of user fees, donations, and souvenir sales to support its activities.

In 1989, for example, the operating budget for the park amounted to $42,000, of which the park will raise about $27,500, or 65 percent of the total, from fees, donations, and sales. User fees of $1 per dive are collected from scuba tour operators and are a major source of revenue. Present projections are that the park will be self-sufficient by 1991, three years earlier than initially expected.

The Saba Marine Park is an excellent example of a mutually beneficial interaction of nature tourism and ecosystem protection. The revenues from tourism will soon be sufficient to cover management costs. Maximum carrying capacity is based more on spatial considerations than environmental concerns; crowding is likely to become a problem sooner than serious environmental impacts from visitation. Although van't Hof estimates the carrying capacity for diving in Saba Marine Park waters at about 80,000 dives per year (representing about 13,000 divers), financial self-sufficiency is reached at about 40,000 dives per year.

The Saba example is clearly a special case. With total Caribbean tourism counts of almost 10 million visitors a year (including both island and mainland destinations), this form of low-impact, nature tourism is not the solution to the economic development goals of many Caribbean Basin countries. Nevertheless, the lessons from Saba and other nature tourism (or scuba diving) destinations indicate how tourism and conservation can serve mutually complementary purposes.

LOGGING AND NATURE TOURISM IN THE PHILIPPINES

Sometimes the threats to nature tourism are direct and readily measured—poaching of elephants for their ivory or encroachment of agricultural fields into protected areas are two examples. In other cases, a nature tourism industry may be harmed by actions that take place at some distance but have effects that are transmitted through the environment. These types of impacts can be just as costly.

One example of the latter, ecosystem-linked impact is occurring in the Bacuit Bay area of northern Palawan, an is-

Figure 6.4.   *Bacuit Bay, Palawan, and Surrounding Drainage Basin.*

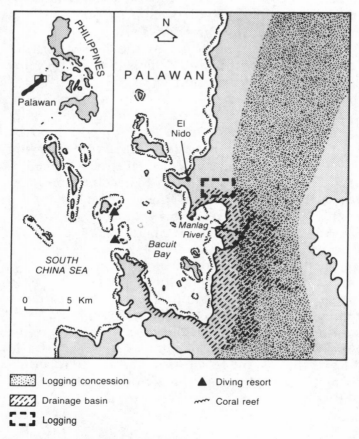

▦	Logging concession	▲	Diving resort
▨	Drainage basin	⌒	Coral reef
⌐⌐	Logging		

Source: *Hodgson and Dixon 1988.*

land in the Philippines (see figure 6.4). Long famous for its beautiful scenery, abundant fish life, and clear water, Bacuit Bay and the small town of El Nido were largely undeveloped until recently. Access was difficult and costly.

Prior to 1979, there was little organized tourism in the Bacuit Bay/El Nido region. Then a Philippine-Japanese joint venture set up a scuba diving resort on a small island at the mouth of the bay. This first resort catered to groups of Japanese divers with smaller numbers of other local and foreign divers. The success of this operation led to the establishment of a second resort, located on an adjacent island, in 1984. Both resorts are selling a fragile, rare commodity: clear, warm waters, abundant coral and fish life, and spectacular scenery. The resorts charge top dollar for their services and have a major interest in preserving the bay's ecosystem.

Local artisanal fishermen share these concerns. The two groups have been working together to protect the bay's coral and fish population to their mutual benefit. Both groups also had an incentive to cooperate with the marine police to enforce the trawler ban in nearshore areas.

A third industry in the area, however, has caused a major resource use conflict. Most of the Bacuit Bay watershed is forested and a portion falls within a concession granted to a major logging firm. In this steep watershed with highly erosive soils, logging results in substantial erosion of that soil, which is deposited directly into the bay. The sediment kills the coral, thereby reducing biomass production and the dependent fishery, and clouds the water. Both the diving and fishing industry suffer as a result and incur major economic losses.

A detailed ecological-economic analysis of the three industries examined the financial implications of continued logging versus a logging ban. Continued logging would result in a loss of a substantial part of the bay's coral ecosystem and the eventual closing of the dive resorts. Fish catch would also be reduced. A logging ban would avoid these costs but would deprive the firm of income from the timber located in the bay's watershed.

Gross revenues were examined for all three industries. A logging ban was estimated to produce over $75 million in revenues over a ten-year period from a thriving tourism ($47 million) and fishing ($28 million) industry. Logging revenue would be zero. Continued logging, on the other hand, would generate $13 million in logging revenues over the same ten years but would result in major decreases in tourism revenue (to $8 million) and fishery income (to $13 million). The "cost" of continued logging, therefore, was about $40 million in gross revenue over the ten-year period. Details of the analysis are presented in Hodgson and Dixon (1988).

The biggest loser would be the nature tourism diving business—not only would planned expansion plans be dropped, but the major resorts would close. Divers would not want to incur the expense and inconvenience of coming to El Nido if the diving were not superb—other sites are available in the Philippines and elsewhere.

The Bacuit Bay/El Nido case is still evolving. Because of political factors, attempts to ban logging have failed to date, but a marine park is being set up in the bay. Whether or not less erosive logging practices can be introduced remains to be seen. In the meantime, the bay ecosystem suffers and tourism is hurt.

THE BOTTOM LINE

We began this chapter with a series of questions about the economics of nature tourism and posed a leading question about "determining if it pays." We believe the answer is that nature tourism is potentially privately profitable as well as socially beneficial. It has the desirable attribute of allowing both conservation and economic development objectives to be met simultaneously.

Nature tourism is not, however, the solution to all conservation problems. Some protected areas cannot sustain any direct use; others may yield larger social benefits when developed for other forms of tourism. Nature tourism will usually be most suitable when areas fall between these two extremes. This includes fragile ecosystems that can accommodate limited numbers of visitors but cannot sustain high use levels; for example, certain coral reef ecosystems or moist tropical forests may not be able to sustain intensive visitor use. This so-called low-impact tourism has important conservation and protection benefits as compared with resort tourism, which is usually more intrusive, even if it yields greater financial benefits.

In other cases, demand, not carrying capacity, may be the limiting factor. Nature tourism is suitable for places that are very remote or difficult to reach, a characteristic that often translates into fairly high costs per visit. Safaris in Africa, or cruises to Alaska or the Galápagos, come to mind.

Nature tourism may also be a desirable alternative when investment funds are limited. Nature tourism frequently uses simpler facilities and has less expensive and less intrusive infrastructure. Thus, it may be practical in cases where funds for large-scale development are not available.

Economic analysis of alternatives is helpful in identifying likely benefits and costs, both private and social, of development options. In some cases, large-scale resort tourism will be the preferred option, in others, nature tourism, with its associated environmental and conservation benefits, may be better. In still other cases, more traditional development or strict protection with no tourism will be the optimal choice. An economic analysis as outlined in this chapter can help clarify the issues, and help determine the potential effects of different alternatives.

REFERENCES

Boo, E. 1990. *Ecotourism: The Potentials and Pitfalls.* Washington, D.C.: World Wildlife Fund.

Brown, G., and W. Henry. 1989. *The Economic Value of Elephants.* LEEC Discussion Paper 89-12. London: London Environmental Economics Centre.

Cicchetti, C. J., and A. M. Freeman III. 1971. "Option Demand and Consumer Surplus: Further Comment." *Quarterly Journal of Economics* 85.

Conrad, J. 1980. "Quasi-option Value and the Expected Value of Information." *Quarterly Journal of Economics* 94.

Dixon, J. A., R. A. Carpenter, L. A. Fallon, P. B. Sherman, and S. Manopimoke. 1988. *Economic Analysis of the Environmental Impacts of Development Projects.* London: Earthscan Publications.

Dixon, J. A., and M. M. Hufschmidt, eds. 1986. *Economic Valuation Techniques for the Environment: A Case Study Workbook.* Baltimore, Maryland: Johns Hopkins University Press.

Dixon, J. A., D. E. James, and P. B. Sherman. 1989. *The Economics of Dryland Management*. London: Earthscan Publications.

Dixon, J. A., and P. B. Sherman. 1990. *Economics of Protected Areas: A New Look at Benefits and Costs*. Covelo, California: Island Press.

Dobias, R. J. 1988. *WWF Contract 3757: Influencing Decision Makers About Providing Enhanced Support for Protected Areas in Thailand (Beneficial Use Project)*. Interim report. Mimeo.

Dobias, R. J., V. Wangwacharakul, and N. Sangswang. 1988. *Beneficial Use Quantifications of Khao Yai National Park: Executive Summary and Main Report*. Bangkok: Thorani Tech for World Wide Fund for Nature.

Frueh, S. 1988. "Report to WWF on Tourism to Protected Areas." Mimeo. Washington, D.C.: World Wildlife Fund-U.S.

Hitzhusen, J. F. 1982. "The Economics of Biomass for Energy." Mimeo. Ohio State University.

Hodgson, G., and J. A. Dixon. 1988. *Logging versus Fisheries and Tourism in Palawan: An Environmental and Economic Analysis*. EAPI Occasional Paper No. 7. Honolulu, Hawaii: East-West Center.

Hufschmidt, M. M., D. E. James, A. D. Meister, B. T. Bower, and J. A. Dixon. 1983. *Environment, Natural Systems and Development: An Economic Valuation Guide*. Baltimore, Maryland: Johns Hopkins University Press.

Krutilla, J. V., and A. C. Fisher. 1985. *The Economics of Natural Environments: Studies in the Valuation of Commodity and Amenity Resources*. 2nd ed. Washington, D.C.: Resources for the Future.

Lindberg, K. 1989. "Tourism as a Conservation Tool." Mimeo. Washington, D.C.: Johns Hopkins University (SAIS).

MacKinnon, J., K. MacKinnon, G. Child, and J. Thorsell. 1986. *Managing Protected Areas in the Tropics*. Gland, Switzerland: International Union for the Conservation of Nature.

McNeely, J. A. 1988. *Economics and Biological Diversity: Developing and Using Incentives to Conserve Biological Re-*

sources. Gland, Switzerland: International Union for the Conservation of Nature.

Mastri, M. 1989. "Dissension Looming over CITES Ban on Elephant Products." *Environment Bulletin* 1, no. 5.

Mathieson, A., and G. Wall. 1982. *Tourism: Economic, Physical and Social Impacts*. London and New York: Longman.

National Parks Division (NPD). 1986. *Khao Yai National Park Management Plan 1987–1991*. Bangkok: National Parks Division, Royal Forest Department.

Posner, B., C. Cuthbertson, E. Towle, and C. Reeder. 1981. *Economic Impact Analysis for the Virgin Islands National Park*. St. Thomas: Island Resources Foundation.

Ray, A. 1984. *Cost-Benefit Analysis: Issues and Methodologies*. Baltimore and London: Johns Hopkins University Press for the World Bank.

Squire, L., and H. G. van der Tak. 1975. *Economic Analysis of Projects*. Baltimore, Maryland: Johns Hopkins University Press.

Thresher, P. 1981. "The Economics of a Lion." *UNASYLVA* 33, no. 134.

Touche Ross Services. 1984. *Kangaroo Island National Parks Cost-Benefit Study*. Adelaide: Touche Ross Services.

van't Hof, T. 1989. "Making Marine Parks Self-Sufficient: The Case of Saba." Paper presented at the Conference on Economics and the Environment, November 6–8, Barbados.

Western, D. 1984. "Amboseli National Park: Human Values and the Conservation of a Savanna Ecosystem." In *National Parks, Conservation and Development: The Role of Protected Areas in Sustaining Society*, edited by J. A. McNeely and K. R. Miller. Washington, D.C.: Smithsonian Institution Press.

Western, D., and W. Henry. 1979. "Economics and Conservation in Third World National Parks." *Bioscience* 29, no. 7.

Western, D., and P. Thresher. 1973. *Development Plans for Amboseli*. Nairobi: World Bank.

CHAPTER 7

Local Participation in Ecotourism Projects

Susan P. Drake

L ocal participation is a necessary component of sustain-able development generally (meeting the needs of present and future generations while protecting the natural resource base) and ecotourism specifically. The term "local participation," as defined here, is the ability of local communities to influence the outcome of development projects such as ecotourism that have an impact on them.

There has been a gradual shift in attitudes of planners and decision-makers over the past two decades toward local participation in the development process. Governments, multilateral development banks, and nongovernmental organizations are beginning to recognize that environmentally sustainable development, of which ecotourism is an example, rests on gaining local support for the project. The capacity of national and local governments to manage effectively the rapidly growing number of development projects and programs will be limited unless functions are decentralized and communities involved. It will be difficult for multilateral development banks and nongovernmental organizations to sustain projects and effectively channel benefits to the local population without the latter's involvement and support. And environmentalists will find it next to impossible to conserve a resource without the commitment of the local population. Finally, pragmatic considerations aside, planners have a moral obligation to listen to the people whom their projects will affect.

There are few, if any, clearly defined approaches to planning local participation for ecotourism projects. However, planners for national parks, wetlands, and river corridor management projects, among others, have obtained local input with varying degrees of success. We will look at a few of these case studies abroad and in the United States and then present a local participation plan for ecotourism projects.

DEFINITION OF LOCAL PARTICIPATION

Local communities can participate in ecotourism projects at the planning stage, during implementation, and can share the benefits. Participation in the planning process includes such tasks as identifying problems, formulating alternatives, planning activities, and allocating resources. Participation in the implementation stage may include actions such as managing and operating a program. Sharing benefits means that the local communities will receive economic, social, political, cultural, and/or other benefits from the project either individually or collectively.

Sam Paul (1987), a World Bank expert on community participation, makes a useful distinction between four levels of intensity in local participation. *Information sharing*—project designers and managers share information with the public in order to facilitate collective or individual action—is the first level. The next level of participation is *consultation*—the public is not only informed, but consulted on key issues at some or all stages in a project cycle. *Decision-making* is the third level—the public is involved in making decisions about project design and implementation. The highest level of intensity is called *initiating action*. This occurs when the public takes the initiative in terms of actions and decisions pertaining to the project.

ADVANTAGES AND DISADVANTAGES

The advantages to incorporating local participation in an ecotourism project are many. First, local participation functions as an early warning system, helping managers to avoid or plan for decisions that might otherwise cause conflict with the local population. Also, including a participation program in the design stage of a project provides the opportunity for the local community to become educated about the purpose and benefits of the project, thereby increasing support for the effort. When managers take the time to listen, they can enlist confidence, trust, and support from the local population. In most cases, people will support a project they understand directly benefits them.

Second, local involvement fosters better planning and decision-making. Conflicts are brought out in the open and resolved during the planning process, additional information is provided that may quantify environmental values, persons previously unrecognized are given a chance to voice their opinion, a wider array of alternatives may be developed from public opinions, and issues, impacts, and management alternatives are better identified.

Third, ensuring local input legitimizes the decision-making process. Accountability of project managers (government or nongovernmental) is reinforced, and local involvement is secured. Other benefits would include possible cost sharing of projects, benefits channeled to the community, and the protection of cultural norms (Hudspeth 1982).

Sam Paul categorizes the benefits associated with local participation as follows:

1. Increasing project efficiency through consultation with people during project planning or involving the public

in management of project implementation or operation.

2. Increasing project effectiveness through greater local involvement to help ensure that the project achieves its objectives and that benefits go to the intended group.

3. Building beneficiary capacity to understand sustainable development by ensuring that participants are actively involved in project planning and implementation and through formal or informal training and consciousness-raising activities.

4. Increasing empowerment by seeking to give the underprivileged sectors of society control over the resources and decisions affecting their lives. It also means ensuring that they receive benefits from the use of the resources.

5. Sharing costs by facilitating a collective understanding and agreement on cost sharing and its enforcement. The public may contribute to labor, financing, or maintenance of the project.

Local participation should not be seen as a panacea for all the socioeconomic costs of ecotourism projects, however. According to Goddard and Cotter (1986) (employees of the U.S. Agency of International Development who have had extensive experience with local participation in development projects), participatory approaches have several disadvantages.

Managing local participation frequently increases the number of managerial and administrative staff required. Pressure is often exerted by the community to increase the level or widen the range of services beyond those originally planned, with consequent increases in project costs. Planners may lose control of a project to opposing forces who seek to use the community organization to wrest control of the project from the implementing agency. Benefits do not always reach the intended target group. Informing local people about a project could increase their frustration or dissatisfaction if the project is delayed or delivers fewer services than planned. In politically volatile areas, the attempt to involve community organizations may create conflicts that either paralyze the project or create much wider problems.

Despite these potential disadvantages, however, the risk of creating an unsustainable ecotourism project—one not supported by the local people, and perhaps destroyed by them—is great if there in no local participation in the project.

The following are examples of different approaches to including public participation in project development.

LOCAL PARTICIPATION IN AMBOSELI NATIONAL PARK IN KENYA

Kenya's Amboseli National Park was one of the first to attempt to incorporate local participation into the implementation of the project. The indigenous population of Masai was represented by the Kajiado District Council. The Council functioned as a channel for the disbursement of tourist revenues generated by the park to the Masai. The benefits to the Masai were to be in the form of management projects such as water wells.

When the scheme was implemented, however, only some of the originally intended benefits from the park reached the Masai. Park revenues went directly to the national government. Funds were then allocated by the Kenyan government to the District Council for management and maintenance of the national reserve facilities. However, the allocated funds never met the amount originally agreed to by the District Council. The projects, therefore, were never funded. This problem could have been resolved, at least partially, by investigating the national political and administrative structure early on in the project as part of the local participation plan.

Sociological and cultural issues such as the Masai's strategies for managing range resources were not thoroughly investigated. In the early management stage of the project, it was discovered that during periods of seasonal drought, the only area with water and therefore wildlife was the area designated to be the reserve. The Masai tired of not receiving benefits promised to them if they stayed off the reserve, and therefore defiantly and purposefully encroached on the reserve in order to hunt its wildlife and let their cattle drink.

Other factors, such as the almost exclusive use of non-Masai as project staff and a perception of the project mission as reforming the cantankerous Masai, exacerbated the situation (Honadle 1985).

Had the Masai been directly involved in the early stages of project planning, and a survey conducted on the social, political, and economic situation of the area, certain assumptions and decisions that negatively affected project management could have been avoided.

COMMUNITY INVOLVEMENT IN GUANACASTE NATIONAL PARK IN COSTA RICA

Costa Rica's dry tropical forests are being restored at the 75,000-hectare Guanacaste National Park (GNP) in the northwest region of the country. One of the primary goals of the project is to promote local involvement in the expansion of the park in order to ensure its long-term viability.

This "enlightened" approach is at least partially due to lessons learned while establishing the Corcovado National Park farther down the coast. People who lived in or around Corcovado were not involved in the formation of the park. Subsequently, gold miners illegally invaded the park, cutting trees, altering watercourses, and dumping sand wastes. They were found to lack awareness that they were destroying the environment. The same people even stated that they supported a strong national park system for Costa Rica.

In Guanacaste National Park, the idea of integrating the local population into the park management system was developed and promoted by Dr. Dan Janzen, the park's founding father. According to Janzen, "It is simply not enough to raise the funds, put a fence around the forest, and call it preserved. The economic and social pressures will inevitably unpreserve it. The challenge isn't what is going to be preserved of tropical forests now, that has already been determined, the challenge is what will be left of tropical forests 100 years from now. It does not matter how much money is put into it, if the people do not understand it and want it, there will not be any national parks 100 years from now. The survival of the forests can be realized only if the soil and its denizens become embedded in the consciousness of the human inhabitants."

Janzen's concept of local participation emphasizes paid or volunteer jobs in park management for local citizens. People from nearby towns live on the outer edges of the park on homesteads owned by the GNP where they can have their own gardens and cows. They are paid park managers and help to fight fires, stop poaching, and plant seeds. Local carpenters are also used to build any infrastructure needed (e.g., bunkhouses for visitors).

Another form of local participation is locally oriented and generated forum discussions about the park and its impact on the local community. These forums are mainly attended by local businessmen and farmers. One, for example, focused on the actions they would take to accommodate the expansion of the park.

Also being pursued is the idea of using local biology teachers as liaisons between park managers and the fishermen on the village civic committees in order to improve the flow of information on relevant issues such as coastal degradation.

Along with environmental restoration, Janzen promotes what he terms "biocultural restoration." The thrust is to embed biological understanding in the local culture by encouraging interaction between the park and its nearly 40,000 neighbors. His goal is to "put biology back into the people's cultural repertoire—back on the same status with music, art, and religion." Toward this end, the regenerated forest is viewed as a library or museum. Plans are in the works to develop educational activities ranging from field trips for local schoolchildren to international symposia. Activities have included hiring a marine biologist to teach schoolchildren in the nearby fishing village about coastal issues, and drawing local people into the park by offering non-paying research technician apprenticeships for forest restoration and inventory projects.

The political, economic, and social environment in Costa Rica and in the Guanacaste region has been very supportive of this participatory approach. Politically, the project has been supported by all levels of government, including the president of Costa Rica and the National Parks Service director.

Economically, few farmers and landholders in the area have resisted selling their land, since most of the farmland in the park is of poor quality. The population is literate, with a diverse lifestyle that includes farming, ranching, fishing, timber extraction, civil service, and small business. The local people are knowledgeable about aspects of park management such as fighting fires, maintaining trails and buildings, herding cattle, identifying and understanding vegetation and trees, and dealing with biotic challenges such as snakes.

According to Janzen, the following elements are essential to the success of sustainable development and ecotourism projects:

1. Base the development of the park on the kinds of habitats that will make the park the most user-friendly (community involvement value, recreational value, interest-generating value, tourist income value, etc.).
2. Restore a tropical national park, because the process itself facilitates community participation in the planning of the park and in the mechanics of its growth, thereby engendering a desire to preserve it aside from its innate or taught attractiveness.
3. Conservation must be based in education. Put natural history back into the human repertoire.
4. Assist the intellectual development of the local people

and increase their understanding of the biological world beyond fields and pastures.

LOCAL PARTICIPATION APPROACHES FOR ENVIRONMENTAL PROJECTS IN THE UNITED STATES

Local participation plans in the developing world will vary from those in the United States due to different relationships with government institutions, nongovernmental organizations, and citizens. Nevertheless, the following approaches to local participation used in United States environmental planning can provide useful guidance in the development of a participation process for ecotourism projects around the world.

LOCAL PARTICIPATION PROGRAM FOR WETLAND PROJECTS

The Environmental Protection Agency (EPA), in conjunction with federal, state, and local agencies, conducts an Advanced Identification of wetlands (ADID) process when it designates wetland areas as suitable or unsuitable for fill material. As part of the planning process, each ADID project manager is encouraged to develop a local participation plan.

A guidance document on how to develop a community relations program for advanced identification efforts was developed by EPA's Office of Wetlands Protection for use by EPA regional offices and local governments.

The objectives of the Advanced Identification Community Relations Program are to: (1) gather information about the community in which the wetlands are located; (2) give citizens the opportunity to comment on and provide their knowledge on aspects of the project; (3) channel discussion or conflict into a forum; and (4) involve other federal, state, and local agencies in joint communications and education efforts.

There are three initial questions considered when an ADID community relations effort is launched. These are: (1) What is the community for the particular ADID project? (2) What are the best ways for learning more about these communities? (3) What are the best routes for reaching the communities with information and/or requests for assistance?

The diversity of communities, interests, ecosystems, and development patterns at different places around the country requires individual evaluations of appropriate community relations strategies for each new ADID project. No single approach is appropriate to all regions, or even to all circumstances in a single region.

There are three major tasks in developing an ADID plan that are closely related to the questions asked above: (1) identifying appropriate agencies, officials, and staff to serve on a coordinating committee for an interagency community relations effort; (2) learning about the community; and (3) identifying appropriate community relations activities and coordinating them with the expected steps in the project.

The program sets forth ways to identify appropriate agencies and officials, including querying state and local government directories, universities, associations, business representatives, and following local press coverage of economic/development issues in the area.

The program recommends the development of a local needs-and-wants survey. Using the lists of identified agencies and individuals and information from the survey, activities and approaches to ensure good community relations are identified. The nature of community concern and the extent of community involvement in the past are also taken into account.

Community relations activities conducted under ADID projects range from briefing state and local officials during the project design stage, developing fact sheets describing the area, known values of the area, history of threats, and benefits from the project, conducting educational presentations, developing and distributing press releases, conducting news conferences to more participatory activities such as holding public hearings, conducting small group meetings, and establishing informal advisory groups.

ADVANCED IDENTIFICATION PROCESS FOR WEST KENTUCKY COALFIELD WETLANDS

In 1989, EPA decided to conduct an Advanced Identification (ADID) study and related Public Involvement Plan for a four-county area in west Kentucky. The ADID was initiated due to the significant impact of coal mining on wetlands in the area. The project goals were to promote public and industry awareness of wetland values through public information dissemination and local participation in the ADID process. The ADID study team collected information on wetlands in the study area. Their preliminary findings were circulated to federal, state, and local agencies for their comments and recommendations.

EPA then developed a public participation and information process that began with a series of one-on-one meetings with key players such as the Kentucky Coal Association and political representatives. Here the parties discussed their concerns and needs, and a preliminary approach was negotiated. These discussions formed the basis for a larger community meeting, which was publicized through the media. Key individuals were sent letters of invitation. At the meeting, the EPA informed the public of the initiation of the ADID study, and explained the ADID analysis and how it would affect the community.

The Kentucky Coal Association helped EPA explain its goals to the community. This helped defuse the potential for individuals to be concerned that wetlands protection might decrease income related to coal.

Some organization representatives gave prepared remarks and then answered questions. EPA responded to some questions orally and others in writing at a later date. The entire meeting was videotaped to ensure all comments were incorporated into the planning process.

EPA distributed three fact sheets: (1) general information on wetlands, and the ADID process, (2) specific wetlands site information, and (3) information aimed at the community affected by wetlands regulation, explaining why wetlands need to be protected. EPA and the Corps of Engineers presented information on the values of wetlands and the ADID process. Both agencies conveyed what they were doing, what and who were going to be involved, and how the community was going to be affected by the effort.

RIVER CORRIDOR MANAGEMENT

The Wild and Scenic Rivers Act authorizes the National Park Service (NPS) to protect free-flowing rivers in their natural state. As an outgrowth of this effort, the NPS has developed the riverwork process, which facilitates local planning and implementation for the conservation of rivers. The public is made a part of the planning process. The effort is initiated by local citizens, nongovernmental or governmental organizations, or by the National Park Service in conjunction with the local or state government. A "greenway plan" or "river corridor management plan" is created as a guide for achieving a desired future, indicating community recommendations for land and water use management within the river area. It identifies the most important features of a corridor, describes the ways in which it can be maintained, and assigns responsibility for its protection and use.

According to Glen Eugster (1988), director of the mid-Atlantic region of the National Park Service, there are nine elements or steps in the planning process:

1. Define the role and function of the river corridor. Bring interests together to discuss the existing and future use of the corridor. Build public and private support, help obtain appropriate state and federal government funds, and coordinate public and private interests.
2. Determine project goals. Seek public input to further develop and refine the goals and objectives of the effort. Public support is seen as critical to the project's suc-

cess. The manager is required to inform the community and build public consensus as early as possible.

3. Initiate the greenway project. Enlist all constituencies in an effort to garner support for the project. Develop a project proposal and establish a project agreement describing project roles, tasks, products, time schedules, and financial arrangements.

4. Involve the public. This step of the local participation plan is designed to build support and develop a constituency for the river project. By involving key area leaders and a broad cross-section of interested individuals and organizations, the manager can ensure that the project goals are relevant to local needs.

5. Assess resources and land use. Place a qualitative value on resources in order to establish priorities for conservation.

6. Analyze local issues and concerns. Identify potential conflicts and work to address local needs and concerns.

7. Explore regulatory and administrative alternatives. Identify governmental programs and resources that can be used to help protect the river corridors.

8. Recruit community leaders. Identify key community leaders such as elected public officials and civic groups and get them involved in the project.

9. Develop an implementation strategy. Using the above information and contacts as a base, develop an action-oriented strategy that will provide specific recommendations on what needs to be done and how.

THE RIVERWORK PUBLIC INVOLVEMENT PLAN

The riverwork approach recommends a two-step process in developing a public involvement plan. The first step is to address the following questions: Who is the public? What do you want from the public? What will you give the public? How much do you want to involve the public? When is public involvement appropriate or most effective?

There are several ways in which the public and other interested groups can be identified (Hudspeth 1982): self-identification, where players introduce themselves on hearing about the project; third-party identification through local citizen committees, environmental groups, or local government agencies identify groups and individuals who should be involved in planning or who are affected by the proposed project; and staff identification through the analysis of associations, general lists, field interviews, affected publics, and geographical information.

The second step in developing a public involvement plan is to choose appropriate techniques for obtaining citizen participation. The riverwork process approach recommends the following techniques (other techniques that may be useful are described in the Appendix):

1. Form an advisory committee or citizens' task force to participate in and oversee the development of a river conservation effort. All interested parties should be included. Its role is to provide direction and information to other local groups and provide technical and political expertise.
2. Conduct meetings (public hearings, workshops, forums, committee meetings) to convey information, report results, share and develop ideas, and help people make decisions.
3. Conduct surveys to elicit ideas and concerns about the river's resources.
4. Conduct personal interviews where issues are complex and where many open-ended questions need to be asked. Personal interviews are some of the best information-gathering tools available, but they take time.
5. Inform mass media of project.
6. Develop newsletters, posters, and other informational materials.

After the key issues and goals are identified and the public involvement program initiated, the public is asked for input on a spectrum of alternatives for resolving resource issues and achieving their goals. Then they are involved in creating an action agenda that determines who is responsible for initiating and implementing each action, how each action will be taken, and when it will be taken.

RIVERWORK CASE STUDY: THE LACKAWANNA RIVER CITIZENS' MASTER PLAN

In 1989, the Lackawanna River Corridor Association (LRCA), founded by Len Altier, set out to restore the Lackawanna River by improving the management of its habitat and recreational opportunities. Altier discussed his board's goals with the National Park Service and decided that they should prepare a citizens' plan using the riverwork planning process.

Prior to the development of the master plan, Altier effected an informal media plan of action in order to build public consensus on the need to restore the river. He met with the managing editor of the largest newspaper in his area and explained the association's objective. The editor agreed to write an editorial on the subject. During the first year of the effort, the paper printed Altier's articles on the issue. Altier also organized weekly status meetings with the newspaper staff. It took one year for the public to become excited about the idea of restoring the river and for dialogue to begin among local citizens.

At that point, Altier sent advertisements to newspapers, TV and radio stations, requesting citizen attendance at a public meeting to discuss the future of the river. The meeting was held in a building close to the river (parking was available!). An outside consultant, recommended by the National Park Service, attended the meeting to explain the value of the river and the need for a plan of action to restore it. Based on the riverwork process, citizens discussed issues such as water quality, habitat loss, and so forth. The National Park Service compiled all the comments into a document that was later used to develop the master plan.

Regular monthly public meetings were established and attended by key leaders from the community. Through this forum, it was decided to develop a citizens' master plan. The National Park Service sent in a professional outsider to assist with its development. After five months of meetings, the

Lackawanna River Association was formally established under Internal Revenue Service (IRS) rules. Following advice from professional river planners, the board of directors of the LRCA recruited two lawyers, two real estate brokers, two corporate executives, and a municipal representative for a formal citizens' committee.

The Lackawanna River Citizens Master Plan was developed with a great deal of local participation. Several data-gathering techniques were used to build an information base for the master plan. The LRCA personnel and area volunteers organized focus groups, conducted individual interviews, played an integral role in public meetings, and reviewed and approved all facets of the project.

LRCA also helped prepare a river and shoreline assessment. The assessment divided the river into sections, each of which was reviewed by a volunteer assessment team. Hundreds of citizens from the community participated on these teams. Each had a specific research responsibility.

Six months were spent conducting a series of focus groups attended by teams of experts and citizens to discuss the issue. These groups included representatives from organizations concerned with land use management, recreation and open space, economic redevelopment, fish and wildlife, water pollution and quality, education, and training. Experts were asked to identify the most important problems facing the river valley and to recommend the most effective programs for overcoming them. Consultants facilitated group discussions, all of which were videotaped. A report on the focus groups was compiled and sent to the press. Subsequently, several sections of the report were printed. It was later used to develop the master plan.

The LCRA solicited additional comments and ideas from the public by conducting a series of individual interviews and holding a series of public meetings at three locations in the river valley. The group presented its study plan and some of its research findings to state and county officials as well as bank presidents, union and commerce officials, and religious and civic groups. Many officials were skeptical of the cost of implementing such a plan.

In response to the skepticism, Altier contacted a key official in the State Department of Community Affairs. The regional director of the department became an adviser to the LRCA. He provided the association with information on available sources of funds for river projects. The association then prepared applications for funding activities along the river.

In order to create public awareness and to continue to build consensus, the association produced a series of public service announcements for TV and radio. They also developed a series of news shows on the river for their CBS affiliate. In addition, they held a town meeting on the river at which experts discussed the issues. It was made into a one-hour live broadcast. The association also developed a twenty-two-minute video of a flyover of the river. This tape is used for on-the-road presentations to special-interest groups.

The master plan is in the process of being implemented with the full support of almost every interest group in the surrounding community.

PLANNING LOCAL PARTICIPATION IN ECOTOURISM PROJECTS

As we have seen, local participation in environment and development projects can help to contribute to the success of the projects. Ecotourism projects are no exception. Ecotourism is based on the conservation of natural resources, resources that are often utilized by the surrounding communities. In order for an ecotourism project to be successful, the local citizens must be made a part of it. They need to help preserve the natural resource for the tourist, and must see a benefit for themselves in doing so.

Following is a new approach to planning for local participation in ecotourism projects. It is based on previously successful and nonsuccessful local participation projects and research into the field as outlined earlier in this chapter.

PHASE I: DETERMINE ROLE OF LOCAL PARTICIPATION IN PROJECT

Examine the goals of the ecotourism project to determine how local participation can best assist the attainment of those goals through improving project efficiency, increasing project effectiveness, building beneficiary capacity, and sharing project costs. Identify local participation goals.

PHASE II: CHOOSE RESEARCH TEAM

A research team for the local participation component of the project should include people who have expertise in sociology and anthropology and who have experience in participatory approaches, as well as those with experience in media and survey research.

PHASE III: CONDUCT PRELIMINARY STUDIES (PREDESIGN STAGE)

Using existing documents, conduct preliminary studies of the political, economic, and social situation of the community and its surrounding environment. This can then be followed by surveys, interviews with families and community leaders, and discussion groups. A political analysis should determine whether there is political support for the democratic principles upon which local participation is based.

The analysis could include any or all of the following components:

1. Assessment of the needs and wants of the community.
2. Identification of the key local leaders and key organizations or groups (industry, environmental groups, unions, etc.). Determine which groups are most powerful within the community. Determine who can best speak for the local citizens and who could be possible participants, facilitators, or managers (of money and land) in the participation process.

3. Identification of major newspapers, TV and radio stations.
4. Assessment of the local community's view of participation in the project. (Is there a history of participation? If so, was the experience positive?)
5. Determination of the capacity and constraints of the local government, village, and nongovernmental institutions in supporting local participation. Identify existing grass roots organizations and determine if there is a need to strengthen existing institutions or to develop new ones.
6. Assessment of the community's traditions (hunting, etc.), including its view on the conservation and use of natural resources, land use principles, water rights, and management of the resources.
7. Identification of the type of people who are likely to participate and why.
8. Assessment of the role of women in the community. Determinations should be made about, for example, their workload, whether they are able to be in leadership positions, and if there is a stigma against men and women being in the same room during an interview.
9. Assessment of who manages the finances.
10. Assessment of who owns land. Distinguish between landowners and squatters, rich and poor.
11. Assessment of cultural values. Determine what incentives could be used to change attitudes about the environment, if necessary.

PHASE IV: DETERMINE LEVEL OF LOCAL PARTICIPATION

This phase should begin with a careful review of the information obtained about the political environment in which local participation will occur. If the local or national government is not supportive of local participation, then the project manager may wish to develop an alternative method to obtain public input, such as the use of intermediaries. This could mean using existing nongovernmental organizations to facilitate local participation or creating new ones.

Where there exists a political and social environment that encourages public participation, the project manager or team should determine the level of intensity needed, and at what stage within the project it should occur.

If the team decides that participation should occur at the lowest level of intensity, where participation is confined to information sharing, then the team need only proceed through phases V and VI as outlined below.

If consultation is the level to be used, where local people will provide feedback on key issues at some or all stages in a project cycle, again, phases V and VI need to be attained.

If the team decides that the local people should have a decision-making role in matters of project design and implementation, the team would continue through all nine phases of this plan.

PHASE V: DETERMINE APPROPRIATE PARTICIPATION MECHANISM

The most appropriate participation mechanism will be determined by the level of intensity of the participation, the nature of existing institutions (governmental organizations, nongovernmental organizations, grass roots citizens'/user groups, district councils), and characteristics of local people (the degree to which they are accustomed to voicing their opinions, educational background, etc.).

INFORMATION SHARING AND CONSULTATION

If it is decided to promote information sharing or consultation, and there does not already exist a participation mechanism, the team could develop a citizens' committee, conduct public meetings, form discussion groups, or hold an educational workshop.

The composition and role of a citizens' advisory committee will differ depending on the project. In many cases, advisory committees will include representatives from all groups interested in the project and not just those directly affected. Its tasks may include the following: establishing and/or commenting on project goals and objectives to ensure they are realistic and provide adequate direction; recommending the type of benefits accruing to the community; educating the local population about the project; and providing technical and political expertise.

Other methods of participation, especially for the consultative level and with an illiterate population, include the formation of small discussion groups in which visual methods such as problem trees (graphic representations of problems with the project) and community maps (a map of the community's cultural, economic, political, and social situation) are used.

At the information-sharing level, popular theater and video presentations can provide a dramatic representation of the project, raising public awareness about the issues.

INVOLVEMENT IN DECISION-MAKING

In projects affecting indigenous people and/or an illiterate population, the participation mechanisms chosen for the "decision-making level" of participation could include using an existing organization headed by a local representative, or if one does not exist, creating one. The functions performed by local councils vary, but they usually include one or more of the following: representing community concerns and providing input on cultural traditions (in the project design stage), enforcing rules (in the implementation and management stage), and distributing or implementing benefits on behalf of the community (in the management stage).

Some project managers choose to develop a tiered participation mechanism for fairly educated communities, such as an advisory committee with a reporting citizens' subcommittee. When this type of participation mechanism is chosen, it is important to work with the appropriate organizations and appropriate levels within the organizations, and ensure that local representatives are able to communicate their concerns to the upper-level committee decision-makers.

If a new mechanism is being developed, the team will need to identify local leaders who can represent the various constituencies in the community. Nongovernmental organizations can be used as a source of identifying local leaders, officials, and agency representatives. They also can be used as external investigators who can support the participation process by facilitating discussion, helping to link the project to local needs, and providing knowledge at the local level.

PHASE VI: INITIATING DIALOGUE AND EDUCATIONAL EFFORTS

Before meeting with community leaders, a dialogue with the press should be initiated. As discussed earlier, building consensus requires a high degree of public awareness. Soliciting support from the press is therefore essential to the success of the ecotourism project, especially if there is no history of local participation.

Interviews with key community representatives should be conducted prior to larger meetings with the general public in order to prepare all parties for their contact with the public, and to work out any problems that may exist.

When interacting with key leaders, the press, or the general public, the ecotourism team should explain the reason for their presence, the goals and objectives of the ecotourism project, and the ways the project will affect the community. Fact sheets should be prepared that describe the project, the known values of the area, the history of threats, and the benefits from the project to the locality, region, and nation. In addition, films, videos, popular theater and other techniques described above and in the Appendix can be effective in building public consensus for the project.

Facilitated by a project team or team leader, workshops or public meetings should be held to identify and prioritize potential problems associated with the ecotourism project, as well as to identify the community's economic and sociocultural needs.

The facilitators would then write a report on lessons learned and recommendations of the meeting and return it to the community for further discussion.

PHASE VII: COLLECTIVE DECISION-MAKING

This is the phase at which participation takes place at its highest level of intensity. All necessary research has been conducted, and the local people have voiced their concerns and wants. The team then presents the findings of the research and the possible recommendations for action and asks the local community for their reactions. If necessary, a negotiating process would begin in which the people and the team would come to a consensus on actions taken in response to the impacts of the ecotourism project.

PHASE VIII: DEVELOPMENT OF AN ACTION PLAN AND IMPLEMENTATION SCHEME

In this phase, the ecotourism team, together with the local community, develops an action plan for implementing solutions for the problems and needs identified by the community.

For example, the needs identified by the community may include increasing standards of living, alleviating cultural impacts, and educating communities about the value of their resources and their culture. Offers made by the team to address these needs might include: (1) purchasing agricultural produce from villages at market rates or on a contractual basis; (2) developing rewards for villagers who donate or lend artifacts to museums developed for the project; (3) developing gift shops, which would be managed by village cooperatives; (4) developing other employment opportunities for local people (e.g., park managers, tour guides, researchers); and (5) developing cultural guides to the host culture. Other actions could include local people developing rules for tourist visits to their village.

The actions determined by consensus could become individual action plans or one action plan. These should then be integrated into the overall master plan for the ecotourism project.

A plan may be needed to strengthen existing institutions or to create new ones for the purpose of implementing projects, such as channeling funds from the ecotourism project to the beneficiaries. Such organizations should begin small and should act on behalf of the local community. The people who make up the organization should support a single style of accountability (financial and otherwise). One financial management style used by development organizations and applicable to local organizations channeling funds for ecotourism projects is the "open management" style. All expenditures, income, receipts, and accounts are routinely published and posted before the community. The community is trained to understand the proceedings and records of the organization so that it can ensure the accountability of its representatives.

PHASE IX: MONITORING AND EVALUATION

Monitoring and evaluation, the final stage of the local participation plan, are often neglected and yet are very important to the success of an ecotourism project. Teams should monitor the implementation of the project and evaluate the effectiveness of its operation. An assessment should be made of how well objectives are being met, and the degree of participation of all groups, among other factors. Using these findings, adjustments can be made to address unforeseen problems or circumstances.

Model Local Participation Plan

I.   Determine local participation goals
II.   Choose research team
III. Conduct preliminary studies
IV.   Determine level of local participation
    If information sharing (go to V and VI and stop)
    If consultation (go to V and VI and stop)
    If decision-making (do all steps)
V.   Determine appropriate participation mechanism
VI.   Initiate dialogue with press/local community
VII. Collective decision-making
VIII. Develop action plan and implementation mechanism
IX.   Monitoring and evaluation of the project

Appendix

Techniques for Ensuring Community Participation

COMMUNITY MAPS

Participants from various parts of the community prepare a graphic representation of the community or of specific aspects of it, such as the economy (production, marketing, consumption, employment, etc.), health, housing, education, recreation, religion, and culture. The goal is to uncover the community's self-perceptions. The results can be used in the planning process or to help evaluate the project. Because participants do not need to be literate, the process can build self-confidence and nurture the creativity of those who utilize it, particularly if they are from the lower socioeconomic end of the scale.

PROBLEM TREES

Especially appropriate with illiterate participants. Make a list of principal problems identified with the project by the community. Then choose a problem whose solution has been identified as a top priority, and place it in the center of the trunk of the tree. Through group discussion, identify the most immediate causes of this problem and related short-term impacts. Place the immediate causes in the shallow roots of the tree and the short-term impacts in the first branches. Then, identify the deeper causes of the problem and place them at the bottom of the roots of tree and place the longer-term consequences of the problem in the secondary branches. Make a list of elements that should be taken into account in preparing a plan of action to solve the problems identified.

GROUP DISCUSSION

Bring small groups of people together for the general purpose of solving problems by sharing experiences, information, and support. The facilitator should help the group to pose problems, identify causes, discuss possible solutions, and evaluate actions.

The discussions will be most effective if the facilitator does the following: creates a situation in which people feel comfortable and free to speak, sing, draw, or perform; builds a sense of trust, support, and solidarity among people who previously had no idea that they shared similar concerns and needs; records the discussion in notes, audiotape, or videotape; and breaks down large groups into small committees that are responsible for specific tasks.

PUBLIC MEETINGS

Open meetings to which all members of a constituency are invited. They vary in terms of depth of discussion and the scope of involvement in decision-making.

This mechanism is useful for the following reasons: it informs the constituency at various stages in the project; it provides an opportunity for all members of the constituency to contribute to the design and implementation of the project; it can obtain and maintain constituency approval and support; and it can interest more constituency members in playing an active role in the research project (encouraging them to join small group discussions, to interview and be interviewed, and to contribute labor and know-how to particular activities).

RESEARCH TEAMS

Local representatives can participate in the research process by joining the research team. They can then ensure that the local citizens are included in planning and that research is carried out democratically.

OPEN-ENDED SURVEYS

Open-ended surveys allow researchers to interview a fairly large number of people using a flexible format that allows the interview to follow the interests of the person being interviewed. The interview may also be conducted with small groups. These surveys help paint a picture of how a large number of people feel about the project and related problems.

COMMUNITY SEMINARS

These are intensive study sessions held among members of one or several communities, and often including representatives from outside institutions such as government agencies, universities, and private community development organizations.

During these sessions, the participants can discuss and analyze the information obtained by the project's researchers in order to plan the next steps. They are able to share information and plan research and action strategies with outside groups.

FACT-FINDING MISSIONS

Group of people from one constituency visit other groups or communities that have been working on similar projects or problems. They can learn about possible funding sources, what can be accomplished, what kind of political, social, and economic obstacles they are likely to face, and what type of time, financial, and community commitments will be needed to make the project a success. In addition, they can exchange information and resources, building a support network across a region or country or even internationally for future activities and for political action.

COLLECTIVE PRODUCTION OF AUDIOVISUAL MATERIALS

Groups produce audiovisual materials such as drawings, photo essays, videotapes, and slide shows that explain and/ or analyze one or more aspects of the project or problem.

This approach provides a form of expression other than words when participants are uncomfortable with words, or when words do not seem to be advancing the research process. Participants learn that audiovisual skills can be acquired by and used by anybody, taking the ability to communicate to a broad audience out of exclusive domain of the mass media.

The shared work experience will often strengthen the group. Most important, it helps to develop a common understanding of the problem through the planning, discussion, and production of a shared statement. Finally, it produces educational materials that can be used to reach out to a larger group.

POPULAR THEATER

Popular theater can speak to people in their own language and deal with problems of direct relevance to their situation. It is an inexpensive method for raising public awareness and is accessible to all socioeconomic classes. As a collective expression and communal activity, it creates an environment for cooperation rather than individual thinking and action. Participants learn from each other rather than from an expert.

REFERENCES

Allen, William. 1986. "Biocultural Restoration of a Tropical Forest." *Bioscience* 38, no. 3.

Amaah-Ofosu, Waafas. 1989. "Hearings on the Food-Population Equation." U.S. House Committee on Science and Technology, Subcommittee on Natural Resources, Agricultural Research and the Environment (February 28).

Anderson, D., and R. Grove. 1987. *Conservation in Africa: People, Policies, and Practice*. Cambridge, U.K.: Cambridge University Press.

Bamberger, Michael. 1986a. "The Role of Community Participation in Development Planning and Project Management." Washington, D.C.: World Bank.

———. 1986b. "Readings in Community Participation." Papers presented at an international workshop organized by the Economic Development Institute at the World Bank, World Bank, Washington, D.C.

Bell, R. H. V. "Conservation with a Human Face: Conflict and Reconciliation in African Land Use Planning." In *Conservation in Africa: People, Policies and Practice*, edited by Anderson and Grove. Cambridge, U.K.: Cambridge University Press.

Corbeth, Margene. 1983. *GreenLine Parks: Land Conservation Trends for the Eighties and Beyond*. Washington, D.C.: National Parks and Conservation Association.

Erickson, D. L., and A. C. Davis. 1976. "Public Involvement in Recreation Resource Decision Making." In *Proceedings of the Southern States Recreation Research Applications Workshop*. USDA Forest Service, Asheville, N.C.

Eugster, J. Glen. 1988. "Steps in State and Local Greenway Planning." *National Wetlands Newsletter*. New York: National Association of Wetlands Managers.

Goddard, Paula, and Jim Cotter. 1986. "USAID's Experience with Community Participation." In *Readings in Community Participation*, compiled by Michael Bamberger. Washington, D.C.: World Bank.

Holden, Constance. 1986. "Regrowing a Dry Tropical Forest." *Science* 234, no. 4778: 809–810.

Honadle, George, and VanSant, Jerry. 1985. "Enhancing Local Action." In *Implementation of Sustainability: Lessons from Integrated Rural Development*. West Hartford, Connecticut: Kumarian Press.

Hudspeth, Thomas R. 1982. "Visual Preference as a Tool for Citizen Participation: A Case Study of Urban Revitalization in Burlington, Vermont." Dissertation thesis, University of Michigan, Ann Arbor.

Janzen, Daniel. 1986. "Guanacaste National Park: Tropical Ecological and Cultural Restoration," Editorial Universidad Estatal a Distancia, San Jose, Costa Rica.

Lackawanna River Corridor Association. 1990. "Lackawanna River: Citizens Master Plan." Prepared by Hoffman, Williams, Lafen, and Fletcher Consultants, Silver Spring, Maryland.

Lamberton, D. M. 1981. "Communication in Development Planning." In Bruce R. Crouch and Shankariah Chamala, eds. *Extension Education and Rural Development*. New York: Wiley.

Little, Peter D., and D. W. Brokensha. 1987. "Local Institutions, Tenure and Resource Management in East Africa." In *Conservation In Africa: People, Policies, and Practice*. Cambridge, U.K.: Cambridge University Press.

Lupanga, Ildefons. 1988. "Promise and Pitfalls—Enlisting Cooperation in Developing Countries." *KIDMA, Israel Journal of Development* 10, no. 39.

Maslow, Jonathan. 1987. "A Dream of Trees," *Philadelphia Magazine*.

Moser, Caroline. 1989. "Approaches to Community Participation in Urban Development Programs in Third World Countries." Washington, D.C.: Economic Development Institute, World Bank.

Nagle, William, and Ghose, Sanjoy. 1989. "Beneficiary Participation in Some World Bank Supported Projects." Washington, D.C.: International Economic Relations Division of the Strategic Planning and Review Department, World Bank.

National Park Service. 1988. *Riverwork Book*. Philadelphia: National Parks Service, Mid-Atlantic Office.

Paul, Samuel. 1987. "Community Participation in Development Projects: The World Bank Experience." Washington, D.C.: World Bank.

Rice, Marilyn. 1988a. "Guidelines for the Development of Participatory Action-Oriented Research Projects." Pan American Health Organization, Health Services Development Program, Health Services Development Series No. 65., Washington, D.C.

———. 1988b. "Social Participation in Local Health Systems." Pan American Health Organization, Health Services Development Program, Washington, D.C.

Salmen, L. F. 1987. *Listen to the People*. Oxford: Oxford University Press.

Sun, Margerie. "Costa Rica's Campaign for Conservation." *Science* 239, no. 4846: 1366–1369.

Thorsell, J. 1984. "Some Observations on Management Planning for Protected Areas in East Africa." In *Proceedings of the 22nd Working Session Commission on National Parks and Protected Areas*. Victoria Falls, Zimbabwe, 27–29 May 1983. Gland, Switzerland: IUCN, 1984.

Trigano, Gilbert. 1984. "Tourism and the Environment: The Club Méditerranée Experience." *UNDP Industry and Environment Office Newsletter*. Paris: UNDP.

U.S. Environmental Protection Agency, Office of Wetlands Protection. 1989. "Community Relations Handbook and Case Studies," *Advanced Identification*, Washington, D.C.

U.S. Environmental Protection Agency, Office of Marine and Estuarine Protection. 1988. *Estuary Program Primer*. Washington, D.C.

Vanderhogt, Gail, and Jane McConnecy. June 9, 1990. *Interviews on Kentucky Oil Field Case Study*. Washington, D.C.: EPA.

Wengert, N. 1971. "Public Participation in Water Planning: A Critique of Theory, Doctrine, and Practice." *Water Resource Bulletin* 7, no. 1: 26–32.

World Wildlife Fund Letter. 1988. "Private Conservation Groups on the Rise in Latin America and the Caribbean." Washington, D.C.: World Wildlife Fund-U.S.

CHAPTER 8

Marketing Ecotourism: Attracting the Elusive Ecotourist

RICHARD RYEL AND TOM GRASSE

In the travel industry, we define ecotourism as purposeful travel that creates an understanding of cultural and natural history, while safeguarding the integrity of the ecosystem and producing economic benefits that encourage conservation.

The long-term survival of this special type of travel is inextricably linked to the existence of the natural resources that support it. Consequently, the travel companies that design, plan, and coordinate ecotourism programs, and the land operators and guides who control activities in the destinations, must share a conservation ethic. This shared ethic provides the framework within which all marketing and traveling should take place and includes several basic components: increasing public awareness of the environment, maximizing economic benefits for local communities, fostering cultural sensitivity, and minimizing the negative impacts of travel on the environment.

Once the conservation ethic is internalized, an effective

164

nature tour operator will develop a marketing plan that identifies potential clients and how best to reach them. At International Expeditions, we have had ten years of experience in marketing ecotourism. Following are some of the highlights of the strategies and techniques we have found to be effective.

A CONSERVATION ETHIC

The key components of an ecotourism conservation ethic are as follows:

1. Increase awareness of nature. Ecotourism should stimulate among travelers and among the inhabitants of the destination an awareness, appreciation, and understanding of the ecosystem and the need for preservation. Many nature-oriented travel programs tend to emphasize the overt spectacles of nature, such as a half-million wildebeest migrating across the Serengeti Plains, plunging cataracts fed by mighty rivers like the Zambezi and Iguassu, or a skin-cutting ceremony of the Ambonwari tribe of Papua New Guinea.

But what of the less apparent, equally fascinating wonders of nature? Can a traveler fully appreciate the interdependent relationships in nature, including man's own vulnerable niche, without examining the environment more completely? If the subtle beauty and balance of nature are not revealed to travelers, how can their experience in the wilderness promote understanding and appreciation of wildlife?

Ecotourism should redefine for the traveler what is sensational. Colonies of leaf-cutter ants marching across the jungle floor holding high their leaf fragment as though it were a green parasol, an unfolding drama in a spider's web, or a flowering epiphyte precariously suspended from a towering mahogany tree should command equal time with vast herds of large mammals and thundering waterfalls.

Ecotourism also should aim to stimulate an appreciation of nature among the local people. They may take for granted

Figure 8.1   *Ecotourists on an expedition to Antarctica watch a group of penguins march across the dramatic landscape of the polar habitat.*

PHOTO: Dick McGowan, Mountain Travel

the marvels of nature that have been a part of their daily lives, yet the preservation of these vital habitats ultimately rests in their hands.

2. Maximize economic benefits for local people.   The prefix "eco" should refer to economics as well as ecology. One of the greatest incentives for conservation among local peoples is to establish tourism as a primary revenue source for the country and local economy, through utilizing the services provided by the host country whenever possible.

At the local level, direct financial awards to the individuals who provide food and accommodations, who share their knowledge of local flora and fauna, and who produce souvenirs and handicrafts are essential. If their livelihoods are based on, or to some degree dependent on, the preservation of habitat, they will be able to avoid other, less sustainable forms of support.

At the national level, government needs to be convinced

that ecotourism will supply a significant amount of foreign exchange in order for them to provide technical and financial support for the protection of parks and reserves. The use of host country airlines, goods, and services will help in this regard.

3. Encourage cultural sensitivity.

3. Encourage cultural sensitivity. The preservation of a nation's cultural heritage, appreciation for the customs and traditions of native peoples and respect for their privacy and dignity, are also essential fundamentals of ecotourism. The presence of tourists is inevitably intrusive to local inhabitants. Fortunately, travelers visiting remote communities are almost always greeted by the warm smiles and the friendly curiosity of the residents. Nevertheless, travelers should be encouraged to be mindful of their status as interlopers. If a group of Masai came wandering down the street of a typical American neighborhood, stopping frequently to stare in awe at people mowing their lawns, washing their cars, playing badminton with their kids . . . how might these residents react?

Ecotourism strives to make travelers aware that trade with local inhabitants represents an opportunity to learn about their traditions and creative skills. Straw market barter may be fun and harmless in Cancun or Freeport, but it is not productive in undeveloped areas or those less frequented by tourists. Ecotourism should endeavor to control the spirit in which the trade of goods is handled by educating tourists regarding the potentially corrupting impact pure barter can have on traditional economies that are based in communal sharing.

4. Minimize negative impacts on the environment. Though the intended outcome of ecotourism is the development of tourism as a sustainable economic resource for the destination, it has a negative impact on the immediate environment. Tourism support facilities translate into hotels and lodges, airports, roads, and waste disposal. Even the seemingly harmless observation of wildlife can have grave implications and must be approached with care by tour operators and their travelers.

Ecotourism must minimize negative impacts on the environment visited while enlightening travelers regarding each habitat's vital role in the balance of nature. For instance, tour operators should not blaze a new trail in the wilderness in order to provide access to an interesting or rare occurrence of nature when existing paths already allow travelers to observe a broad spectrum of wildlife elsewhere.

Many tour operators realize the effects visitation can have on the ecosystem. They know how to minimize the detrimental impact tourism has on wildlife and they maintain rigorous standards as a result of their love and respect for nature; if they do not, they should not operate tours in these areas.

Ecotourism operators often are learned naturalists either through formal education or through field experience. It does not require a great deal of insight on their part to realize that their immediate prosperity and future rely on the preservation of the natural wonders that lure travelers in the first place.

The travel company contemplating an exceptionally delicate area as a destination may determine that a particularly fragile condition exists either in terms of the wildlife population or the indigenous human population that would make visitation too harmful or corruptive. Regardless of accessibility for tourism and its potential value to a travel company or local economy, attracting travelers to such a destination would be irresponsible.

MARKETING ECOTOURISM

DETERMINING MARKETABILITY

What makes a potential ecotourism destination marketable? Destinations can be evaluated on two basic levels: the attraction for travelers and the tourism infrastructure.

Biodiversity is the most important attribute of an ecotourism destination in terms of its attraction for travelers. Areas with an abundance and variety of flora and fauna are alluring subjects for prospective ecotourists. Environments such as the tropical jungles of the Amazon hold the promise of an unforgettable adventure. Prolific biodiversity is not limited to the tropics, however. It can also be discovered in the extreme northern and southern latitudes from Alaska to Patagonia.

Unique geography can also attract tourism to remote and delicate environments. Amid the breathtaking Himalaya Mountains, Nepal beckons tens of thousands of travelers each year. Ayer's Rock, the mammoth sandstone monolith in Australia's desert outback, has been an object of admiration since first encountered by aborigines some 40,000 years ago.

Cultural history is an important factor in a destination's marketability. The opportunity for travelers to experience cultural traditions will increase greatly their enjoyment of the destination. In Papua New Guinea, for example, the visitor will find a myriad of tribal cultures, customs, and artifacts, in addition to the island's beautiful rain forests and wildlife. The Petén in Guatemala boasts a treasure trove of ancient Mayan ruins, and rich Indian culture, amid a unique tropical environment.

A tourism infrastructure must be in place, or put into place, if visitation is to occur. A destination cannot be marketed by an environmentally conscious travel company unless it has adequate accommodations and ground transportation, guides who are able to interpret natural and cultural history, proper access to natural habitats, and cooperative local or national governments. The area must also have tour operators who are receptive to the fundamentals of ecotourism.

A MARKETING STRATEGY

A deep understanding and acceptance of the conservation ethic described earlier is essential when developing marketing initiatives such as those that follow.

Group travel. Most ecotourism expeditions are conducted in small groups consisting of five to thirty participants. This type of travel allows operators to establish an annual travel calendar through negotiations with airlines and hotels to block space for the tour dates. This provides prospective travelers with a varied choice of guaranteed departure dates and reasonably priced packages. A predetermined schedule of trip departures permits the operator to offer complete trip packages at set, all-inclusive prices and arrange outstanding itineraries designed to address the fundamentals of ecotourism. Thus, from the standpoint of both the traveler and the ecotourism operator, this represents the best approach to offering a superior nature travel product.

The advantages of marketing ecotourism in the format of group travel positively outweigh any alternative, despite the rare but inevitable displeasure experienced by the misplaced traveler who becomes uncomfortable amid the enchanting rusticity and unpredictability of an ideal nature travel destination.

Defining the market. Because ecotourism programs are conducted in small groups, it is important to attract people who will enjoy the product after it is purchased. The attitude of one traveler in a small group can significantly influence its other members, and repeat travelers are an important source of income.

Who are these so-called right people? Are these key prospects for ecotourism "born" or "made"?

The answer is both. To narrow the target only to those people predisposed to nature travel ("born" ecotourists) would not be fully productive. These individuals already have a strong interest in exploring the natural wonders of the world. They possess a built-in appreciation for natural history and the desire to preserve wildlife and traditional culture. Certainly, a nature travel experience would serve to nurture this attitude and further the aim of ecotourism. But, in order to fulfill its mission and to achieve business success, ecotourism must also reach out to potential consumers unfamiliar with the concept. Therefore, the ecotourist must be made as well as born.

Potential ecotourists are identified and wooed through a marketing strategy that limits the advertising and communications to a qualified target market in order to achieve cost effectiveness and profitability. Travel companies cannot waste scarce dollars and valuable time communicating the benefits of ecotourism to unqualified consumers.

First, the ecotourism company will need to identify the demographic, psychographic, and geographic characteristics of the desired group. Demographics are factors such as age, sex, race, household income, education, occupation, and family size. Psychographics are lifestyles, beliefs, and other cultural variables. The geographic characteristics of the target market refer to the areas of the country in which there are concentrations of qualified prospects.

Demographically, the key prospects for ecotourism are men and women forty-five to sixty-five years of age; some 58 million Americans age fifty-plus dominate pleasure travel and tourism. They travel more frequently, go longer distances, and stay longer than other groups. The majority have obtained a college degree and many have a postgraduate degree. The occupations of these key prospects range greatly, though most are professional, and their household income and buying power is high. The amount of leisure time at their disposal is great, as many are financially independent and retired.

The vast majority of international ecotourism consumers are North American, European, and Japanese. However, the correlation between ethnic origin and the propensity toward environmentally sensitive travel is more a function of economy than anything else. Citizens of the modern industrialized world have more time, money, and freedom to travel than other cultures.

Psychographic descriptions of purchasers are useful because demographic descriptions do not discriminate well enough between consumers. For example, an electrician may be reported in the same income class as a college professor, but their lives and purchasing habits may be vastly different. Therefore, it is important to go beyond demographics, especially when it comes to making marketing decisions.

The psychographic characteristics among the target market for ecotourism are quite distinctive. The Axiom Market Research Bureau, Inc., has developed a series of twenty adjectives designed to elicit the self-conceptions of respondents in surveys, which can be helpful when identifying a market. Those adjectives that describe the ecotourist include "amicable" (amiable, affable, and benevolent), "broad-minded" (open-minded, liberal, and tolerant), "intelligent" (smart, bright, well-informed), "self-assured" (confident, self-sufficient, secure), and "sociable" (friendly, cheerful, likable). By now, anyone reading this who has ever participated in an ecotourism expedition should be sufficiently flattered!

Though more and more magazines, newspapers, and broadcast media are providing prospective advertisers with psychographic profiles of their audiences in addition to detailed demographic information, the marketers of ecotourism must often rely on experience and intuition when making a decision to purchase advertising space in a previously untried medium.

Geographically, concentrations of key nature travel prospects are found in the northeast United States (New York, Boston, Washington, D.C., etc.) the West Coast (Seattle, San Francisco, Los Angeles, etc.), and in major cities elsewhere like Chicago, Dallas, and Denver. These are prosperous areas that attract and support the greatest number of professional occupations. They also support educational institutions such as colleges and universities, museums, zoos, aquariums, planetariums, botanical gardens, and libraries that nurture a curiosity about the natural and cultural history of the world.

Advertising: getting the message out. Once the demographics, psychographics, and geography of the target audience are defined, the company should determine which advertising media to utilize. A company and its product will immediately inherit a measurable degree of trust and acceptance among consumers simply by virtue of their presence in the right advertising medium.

Specialized magazines that are well established and affiliated with highly respected, internationally recognized organizations such as the National Audubon Society, the

Sierra Club, American Museum of Natural History, the Smithsonian Institution, and the Archaeological Institute of America are a prime source of advertising. Other magazines such as *E Magazine, Buzzworm,* and *Geo,* which are not affiliated with special institutions, can also target ecotourism prospects effectively. Upscale travel magazines like *The National Geographic Traveler* or Condé Nast's *Traveler* can be useful if the budget allows. The newspapers of most major cities publish special travel supplements each spring and fall; these too should be considered.

Identifying a key interest common to most ecotourism prospects can help a travel company find effective advertising channels. For example, most nature tourists are active amateur photographers. Therefore, a publication such as *Outdoor Travel & Photography* could prove worthwhile.

In addition to the primary advertising vehicles described above, positive results also can be obtained through the use of supplemental media. Special travel itineraries offered by the company may require targeting advertising to special-interest magazines, for example. A coral reef diving expedition to Belize could be effectively advertised in *Skin Diver* magazine. A different itinerary to Belize, coinciding with Garifuna Day (celebrating a specific ethnic group and its history), could solicit response if advertised in *Native Peoples* magazine. Exploring the archaeological sites of Cuzco and Machu Picchu would certainly appeal to readers of *Archaeology* magazine, while attending the Pushkar camel fair in India might excite the readers of the *New York Times Sophisticated Traveler.*

Ecotourism companies realize maximum results by maintaining a constant presence in the primary media they use. Frequency leads to recognition and top-of-mind awareness. Nature travel companies should therefore invest in repeated advertising with their most productive advertising media. Frequency contracts with media earn special discount rates.

However, an ecotourism operator can rarely afford a schedule of full-page ads in national magazines, which, even in specialized publications having a circulation of only 400,000 to 500,000, can cost more than $10,000 an issue.

There are certain months of the year when people are less likely to travel and response to advertising drops dramatically. During these "down" periods, ecotourism advertisers might consider taking a brief hiatus from advertising in one or two of their primary media.

Ecotourism operators do not always have to carry the full burden of advertising costs. Most airlines and many of the more established lodge operators will provide coop advertising funds to travel companies that feature their services in the ad.

Advertising that complements editorial content also enhances the effectiveness of advertising. Many of the magazines used by nature travel advertisers feature natural history or travel subjects. Operators can thereby reach prospects while their interest is piqued. Ecotourism companies should keep abreast of upcoming editorial coverage in order to take advantage of special features that focus on their destinations. Newspaper travel supplements, magazines, and other media can provide advertisers with editorial calendars.

Crafting the message. Financial constraints often limit nature travel companies to a relatively subtle presence in advertising media. In order to capture attention and induce action, they must ensure that their advertisements are strategically placed both within the magazine and on the page, and that it is creatively designed and written. They should try to maintain a consistent positioning strategy, ad design, use of color, and photographic or illustrative mood in order to draw attention and establish recognition.

The most difficult challenge of advertising ecotourism is the development of effective copy. This is difficult to do within the confines of a tiny display ad, particularly because the inclusion of mandatory information such as the company name, address, and telephone number, the destination or destinations being promoted, the trip price and items not included in that price, often leave little room for enticing prose.

Consequently, the primary advertising objective of most

nature travel companies is to encourage their audience to request additional information about the featured destination by telephone. If the ad successfully accomplishes that objective, captivating brochures describing the destination in detail, projecting vivid images of the wildlife and culture of the habitat, and expressly or implicitly addressing the concept of ecotourism can be mailed to the inquirer.

Creating a mailing list. A valuable outcome of well-targeted, direct response advertising is the creation of a strong mailing list. Mailing lists generated from response to the ecotourism company's own advertising generally means the names and addresses obtained are those of qualified ecotourism prospects. The respondents read the publication in which the company advertises, so the likelihood is great that their demographic and psychographic profiles complement those of the company's target market. They are at least contemplating a nature travel vacation. And if the ad was classified, or positioned in the travel section of the publication, the respondent might be actively planning a trip. Finally, the price of the trip, if it was advertised, did not discourage response.

The resulting mailing list becomes a powerful marketing tool. It allows the company to provide key prospects and past travelers with brochures, newsletters, updates on new destinations, even Christmas cards, the vast majority of which will be examined thoroughly and appreciatively by the recipients. A high-quality assortment of travel brochures provides the operator with an important competitive advantage.

Most traditional travel brochures are designed to fantasize, romanticize, and aggrandize to the point where the reader is mesmerized and hypnotized. They can be brilliantly contrived fables of lavish detail depicting opulent quarters, omnipresent valets, sumptuous feasts, breathtaking panoramas, torrid love affairs, and deep-brown tans.

Ecotourism takes a very different angle toward promotion. To appeal to their most desired prospects, ecotourism marketers present the inherently astounding facts about the destinations they offer. The visual images within the brochures are never meticulously staged shots featuring voluptuous models and caviar molds; instead, they are peeps at nature frozen in time, such as a newly hatched lotus bird testing its gangling legs for the first time or a traveler on an elephant's back within a few feet of a grazing rhinoceros.

Ecotourism operators use brochures in a variety of ways. The most effective method is to offer travel prospects a visually attractive annual travel catalog or digest supplemented by more detailed, destination-specific brochures. The catalog features all of the company's current destinations with a broad description of sights and activities. Prices and a calendar of departure dates are included in the digest. Often, it is produced in an elaborate magazine format with a captivating photographic cover design. A catalog that earns a place on someone's coffee table or an equally accessible and conspicuous place is infinitely more effective than a brochure placed in the trash after a cursory examination.

Brochures specific to each destination offered by the ecotourism operator can greatly enhance and supplement the annual catalog. Smaller operators may use these more descriptive brochures exclusively. The travel brochure often represents the first opportunity the ecotourism operator has to educate the prospective traveler. It is here that the travel company enjoys an ample quantity of time and space to communicate its purpose and the unique qualities of its destinations. In the following excerpt from an ecotourism brochure for Venezuela, it is an inspired naturalist who promises an unforgettable experience in this South American paradise.

> Crossing the heart of Venezuela from the Orinoco Delta to the Andes Mountains is a vast grassland prairie known as the Llanos. Representing about one-third of the total area of Venezuela, this region abounds with the most spectacular wildlife found in South America. Geologically, the Llanos is the bed of an ancient inland sea. The soils are relatively poor and support little vegetation other than grasses—except along the many streams and rivers where

a distinctive type of growth, known as gallery forest, forms dense thickets. Traditionally used as grazing land, the Llanos has a very low population density that contributes to the incredible abundance of wildlife. During the dry season (November–May), the shrinking waterholes attract thousands of animals, including those normally difficult to observe like the Capybara, Giant Anteater and Spectacled Caiman. The number of birds is simply mind-boggling. Within one's field of view it is possible to see, simultaneously, all three New World Storks, eight species of Ibis, Rufescent Tiger Heron, White-faced Whistling Duck and Black-collared Hawk, while smaller birds flit in and out of the scene. . . .

It does not matter whether or not the reader has ever heard of a white-faced whistling duck or a spectacled caiman, only that he or she becomes interested in the prospect of traveling to this remarkable habitat to see such wonders. This ecotourism brochure describes the trip, beginning with an introductory paragraph on the country. It proceeds to discuss each unique habitat to be encountered on the expedition; the Caribbean coastal region, the Llanos, the Guayana Highlands, the Andes Mountains, and the Orinoco Basin. Conspicuously positioned on the back cover is the company's long-standing purpose: "to stimulate an interest in, develop an understanding of, and create an appreciation for the great natural wonders of our Earth."

Dominating the visual aspect of the brochure is a pictorial of Venezuela that includes a wedge-headed capuchin monkey perched on a high limb, a close-up of an exotic rat's tail orchid, and an almost surreal wide-angle view of La Gran Sabana.

Details regarding meals and accommodations are seldom given in these brochures (unlike more traditional tourism materials), although such information is covered thoroughly in other predeparture materials. Lodging on ecotourism expeditions is usually simple and always pleasantly adventuresome. Meals are almost exclusively of the local cuisine.

The travel company wants to prepare travelers fully for

the ecotourism experience, in part because a dissatisfied traveler is bad for business. To this end, the operator will supply a great deal of additional information beyond the destination brochure.

A HYPOTHETICAL EXAMPLE

In order to understand the sequence of events leading to the selling of the nature travel product, let us examine the process through a light-hearted, hypothetical example.

Winston DeBardelben is a forty-eight-year-old lawyer who lives in Albuquerque, New Mexico. One of his hobbies is bird-watching; he even owns a pair of Bausch & Lomb 8 X 42 Black Armored binoculars that he stores under the seat of the Jeep Wagoneer he bought before the kids went off to college. He keeps a stack of magazines on his bedside table and browses through one or two every night before going to sleep. One of his favorite magazines is *Audubon*. While flipping its pages one evening, he notices an attractive, four-color ad with the headline "World Leader in Nature Travel." The long, skinny ad on the left-hand column of the left-hand page features an intriguing photograph—the silhouette of an exotic creature with spiraling antlers, set against a striking orange sunset. "Isn't that a black buck?" he asks himself, recalling a program on India he had seen recently on public television.

As Winston gazed over the dozen or so destinations listed in the ad, he realized that a few of the trips cost about the same as his binoculars. Then he began to imagine himself somewhere in India, peering at a distant stork rookery. Glancing at his sleeping wife, he remembered that she had threatened to take a week's vacation to the Sierra Nevadas with her friends if he didn't come up with a better alternative. She even figured out how much it would cost; all he could recall was that it was four figures. "That settles it," he decided silently. "I'm going to look into this."

The next morning, he called the toll-free number in the ad. His first conversation with the travel company representative was brief. She took his name, address, work and home phone number. She asked where he had seen the ad and whether or not he had ever requested information from the company before. When he replied "No, I haven't," she told him he would be sent a complete catalog of all the destinations available, as well as a brochure on the India expedition.

Less than a week later, Winston received the materials. The fifty-two-page catalog reminded him of some of the magazines he received. With great yearning, he studied the catalog page by page. Then he picked up the eighteen-page, four-color brochure devoted entirely to the company's India expedition. It provided him with facts about the country that piqued his interest and the vivid wildlife photographs appealed to more than just his sense of sight. A day-to-day itinerary, general information and conditions, and a reservation certificate were included as well. The impressive materials gave him a sense that he had contacted a very able company.

When his wife reminded him that it was 7:00 and they were to meet their friends at a local bistro at 7:30, Winston realized that he had spent the better part of an hour gazing at the brochures and daydreaming about a trip to India. Finding it impossible to contain his excitement any longer, he walked over to his closet, hung up his suit, put on a pair of khaki trousers, slipped on his beloved but abused eleven-year-old Sperry Topsiders, walked out into the bedroom, stood before his wife, and announced "Honey, we're going to India this fall!" They celebrated with champagne at the bistro.

As soon as they got home, Winston filled out the reservation certificate and stuck it in an envelope with a deposit check to reserve space on the departure date he had selected.

The next day, Winston called the travel company with a few specific questions. He was impressed by the young woman with whom he spoke. She was a "destination coordinator," and India was her specialty. He was struck by the breadth of her knowledge regarding the natural and cultural history of the country and the fact that she had done archaeology fieldwork in Central America. She recommended that he read a few books on India, particularly one on India's tiger preserves written by a renowned Indian naturalist with whom, he was told, he would meet on his trip. The destination coordinator described some of the remote lodges where he and his wife would stay and what to expect in general.

On receipt of his reservation form, the company mailed Winston a confirmation package consisting of a welcome letter from the company founders and a booklet on the destination featuring historic background, customs, description of habitats, geography and wildlife, information about local currency, shopping tips, and more. The package contained visa applications and a personal health form. There was also a form for him to complete regarding his special interests and a list of suggested readings. Next, Winston received his invoice for the trip. Approximately thirty days prior to leaving for India, the DeBardelbens received their predeparture package. It contained a personal letter telling who would greet them at the destination and other final details. Their airplane tickets were enclosed along with a brief itinerary, customs information, and the names, addresses, and phone listing of their fellow passengers (some of whom would become close friends). An embossed suede passport holder, ticket holder, and leather luggage tags were included, the latter so their bags could be easily identified by porters.

Additional Elements in a Marketing Strategy

This example has demonstrated that good advertising, effective collateral material, expert personal communication, and thorough procedures can go a long way toward making a marketing effort successful. However, there are additional factors in the total marketing "mix" that contribute to awareness and promote participation in ecotourism.

Special group travel. Ecotourism has a special appeal for zoos, museums, aquariums, nature centers, and environmental organizations. These institutions have begun to recognize the potential for educating their members about conservation issues through nature travel, and many of them have full-time travel coordinators on staff. The National Audubon Society, for example, employs a staff of professionals that works closely with nature travel companies in arranging trips for their membership. They use the travel opportunities to educate their members about environmental issues worldwide, and have produced a set of guidelines for environmentally sensitive travel.

The travel company can best demonstrate its overall quality and its commitment to environmentally sensitive ecotourism by offering familiarization tours to group representatives, with the hope that their institutions will choose to travel with the company in the future.

Once a group and an ecotourism operator agree to work together, the operator can provide many forms of marketing support, such as high-quality audiovisual presentations for the group's members and the public. People are encouraged to attend these previews through announcements in the organization's newsletter, special invitation, or a brief note in the local newspaper, perhaps in a calendar of upcoming cultural events. The ecotourism operator may also produce direct mail fliers for the institution to mail to its membership list. Some groups manage to realize additional financial benefits by structuring donations into the price of the trip.

Media coverage.   The 1990s have been dubbed "The Decade of the Environment," and there is growing interest among media in conservation issues. The subject of nature travel alone has an enormous degree of human interest; combined with public concern for the global environment, ecotourism has extraordinarily strong media appeal. Ecotourism operators must treat opportunities for editorial exposure with careful thought and preparedness.

Publicity can result in valuable commercial exposure at little or no cost. But the ecotourism operator must be able to communicate to the media a precise meaning of ecotourism. Reporters are human and may misconstrue ideas if not presented in a clear and concise fashion. To assure that the ecotourism "story" is communicated with accuracy, a public relations plan is essential.

The formulation of a purpose statement is the first step. The purpose statement upon which International Expeditions, Inc., was founded has played an important role in its initial decade of operating ecotourism programs, and has helped it attain a credible image with the news media. Its purpose "is to stimulate an interest in, develop an understanding of, and create an appreciation for the great natural wonders of our Earth."

Travel to exotic locales is a powerful leveraging tool with the media and prospective promotion partners. Trading trips for valuable media can gain exposure for the ecotourism operator that it might otherwise be unable to afford.

Special promotional events. Promotions such as radiothons, workshops, and competitions are a unique, cost-effective way to generate consumer excitement and expand the message of ecotourism to a wider audience. Ecotourism operators should select high-profile partners that have clients with similar demographics (for instance, a popular sport optics manufacturer). Through this cooperation, the ecotourism operator can gain credibility, enhance its image, and broaden awareness for its travel products.

For example, an ecotourism operator and a major rain forest conservation organization recently launched a productive promotional effort in the form of a radio raffle. The top prizes were free expeditions to the Amazon rain forest. An investment of trip costs on the part of the nature travel operator translated into print and broadcast exposure in five major cities and donations in excess of $400,000 for rain forest ecology.

Conscientious support of environmental causes almost always enhances a travel company's image. While profit is not the primary motive, this support sometimes results in immediate response and increased sales.

International Expeditions has been involved with a cooperative promotional effort entitled the "International Rainforest Workshop." Participants in the workshop will travel to the Amazon and Napo rivers, where some of the foremost experts on rain forest ecology guide travelers through an intensive, week-long exploration of the forest. The tour company's partners include the Peruvian Foundation for the Conservation of Nature (FPCN), the Nature Conservancy, and Exploraciones Amazonicas, an environmentally sensitive lodging operator that will host the annual event. There are no prerequisites for participation besides a love and enthusiasm for the rain forest. A major portion of the funds generated will be used for the development of the Amazon Center for Environmental Education and Research (ACEER). The center will provide environmental education and a study area for researchers, who will in turn share their knowledge and experience with visitors.

Special projects like this accomplish many objectives. First, the experience will change the lives of over 100 participants to some degree. Appreciation and understanding even beyond that normally associated with an ecotourism experience will be realized among these travelers.

The local community will benefit as well. They will learn more about their environment and nature tourism. Money will be generated by the event, profiting local interests and leading to the development of the research center, which will be utilized by many scientists and ecotourists who will spend money in the community.

BELIZE: A CASE STUDY

In 1980, the year International Expeditions was founded, the Caribbean country of Belize situated on the northeast coast of Central America was mostly virgin territory. Only its outlying coral islands supported tourism, attracting divers and sport fishermen. Soon after International Expeditions began operations, Belize was selected as a potential ecotourism destination for the company. Steve Cox, one of the company's founders, traveled to Belize in order to evaluate the tourism infrastructure and examine the marketing viability of the destination, particularly the country's interior.

At that time, roads were bad and Land Rovers were needed to access most areas. Ecotourism lodging on the mainland was extremely limited and unable to accommodate more than a few dozen intrepid travelers. There were few trained guides. Yet the essential elements of a wonderful nature travel destination were there—biodiversity and the potential to develop an acceptable tourism infrastructure. It also seemed apparent that ecotourism would be able to safeguard this unspoiled paradise.

International Expeditions set out to improve or help establish adequate infrastructure in such ecologically diverse areas as Crooked Tree and Mountain Pine Ridge in the northwestern and central parts of Belize. Gradually, more travelers were brought to natural history sites in Belize, but only as many as the current tourist infrastructure could comfortably support.

As the few existing lodge owners realized the great revenue potential represented by International Expeditions and nature travel in general, plans were set into motion for the expansion of existing accommodations, construction of new lodges, and the advancement of environmentally sensitive tourism. Chaa Creek, located on the Macal River in the foothills of Mountain Pine Ridge, was just a simple two-room facility in 1980. Today, it has grown to become a prosperous resort of fourteen thatched-roof cabanas, a relaxing open-air bar, a quaint little gift shop featuring local arts and crafts, and a spacious dining terrace serving local cuisine.

Once a one-dimensional travel destination that focused on diving and fishing, Belize has become recognized as a multifaceted paradise, and the tourism industry is growing rapidly. The government has recognized the importance of this revenue source through establishing a Ministry of Tourism and the Environment, which is promulgating a policy of conservation and controlled tourism development.

In addition to governmental support of ecotourism, local inhabitants are beginning to realize benefits from nature travel. The population of Belize is small, approximately 170,000, so even the relatively modest revenue that ecotourism currently represents is felt among all levels of society.

The Community Baboon Sanctuary ("baboon" is the local name for the black howler monkey) is an inspiring example of how ecotourism can work to the benefit of nature, local communities, and private interests. The black howler monkey has been threatened by loss of its forest habitat to slash-and-burn agriculture. To combat this problem, local farmers and landowners started a grass roots conservation effort in the form of a Community Baboon Sanctuary at Bermudian Landing, with help from the Belize Audubon Society, the World Wildlife Fund, and others. The sanctuary attracts a significant volume of travelers, and the monetary benefits accrue to both the sanctuary and the community. For example, a group of local women is paid to prepare meals for travelers visiting the sanctuary by companies like International Expeditions.

Belizians see ecotourism as the wave of the future. Meb Cutlack, editor of the *Belize Review*, wrote this about it:

> The key word for Belize's future is ECOTOURISM because not only is ecotourism the world's fastest growing area of the tourism industry but it is essentially the way in which Belize can earn enormous revenue from her natural resources and simultaneously husband and care for those resources . . . her reef, cays, rain forest, rivers, streams, Mayan ruins, wildlands and wildlife. There are times when infrastructure development, the building of hotels, roads, boat docks, and other essentials for tourism will challenge the concept of pure conservation—just as essential agricultural development will at times present a challenge. But such conflicts are surmountable with wisdom and goodwill. It is not a matter of "development at any cost" but "sustainable development which respects man and nature." (Cutlack 1990)

CONCLUSION

The marketing of ecotourism is a complex challenge. Success is not measured simply by company profits. It relies on a much greater efficiency of resource use. The ecotourism operator must consider variables that transcend purely monetary concerns.

Education of travelers by both instruction and example is as critical to success as providing a comfortable, fun, and hassle-free experience. Generating revenues for the country and local communities is also essential. And, finally, the highest goal must be the conservation of the fragile ecosystems that comprise the nature tour experience.

REFERENCE

Cutlack, M. 1990. *Belize Review* (May).

CHAPTER 9

Making Ecotourism Sustainable: Recommendations for Planning, Development, and Management

ELIZABETH BOO

World Wildlife Fund (WWF) recently completed an evaluation of the current status of ecotourism worldwide, and its economic and environmental impacts (Boo 1990). The research focused on Latin America and the Caribbean, with case studies in Belize, Costa Rica, Dominica, Ecuador, and Mexico, though the findings are likely to be applicable elsewhere.

The study confirmed the presence of a growing demand for ecotourism. Where data were available, records of visitor counts were collected at case study sites. Almost invariably, numbers of domestic and international ecotourists were seen to be rising rapidly. Tour operators and travel agents were interviewed about travel trends. All reported a great shift in client demand toward nature tours, despite a minimum of marketing and promotion. In addition, surveys con-

187

ducted at airports showed a large percentage of randomly interviewed tourists were there for the nature. Some 46 percent cited natural areas as the primary or very important reason for their decision to travel. Six in ten (57 percent) stated that they visited at least one park during their stay.

We concluded, however, that the potential benefits of ecotourism, both economic and environmental, are yet to be realized. The vast majority of parks are not in a position to gain financially from tourism because they do not provide adequate means for tourists to spend money. Most parks lack trained guides, interpretive information, entrance fee systems, and basic infrastructure such as visitor centers. Significant opportunities to bring money into the park and to provide employment for local populations are missed.

Another lost opportunity is the education of visitors. Tourists experiencing a natural area directly are more apt to become involved in conservation if informed about the issues. Unfortunately, most parks do not have the personnel or programs available to educate tourists.

At the same time that the benefits of ecotourism are untapped, the potential economic and environmental costs have not been fully understood or monitored. Most international travel agents and tour operators have yet to establish relations with local counterparts, and there is no assurance that a portion of the financial gains from ecotourism benefits the local community. Also, mechanisms are not in place to thoroughly evaluate the environmental consequences of tourism. Few studies have been done to monitor changes and to determine carrying capacities for parks. Yet this information is critical to the healthy growth of the ecotourism business.

The study clearly highlights the importance of including local people in the planning, development, and management of ecotourism. Many of the parks and reserves in developing countries being discovered by nature travelers are surrounded by native populations who are dependent on the natural resources of the area for their livelihood. In order to stem the growing pressure from development activities and conserve the natural resources, the native populations must be offered viable alternatives to use the resources in sustainable ways. Ecotourism is one such option.

The process of involving local communities in ecotourism projects and simultaneously protecting natural resources is not easy. Local people are often widely distributed over a large geographic area and are not part of any established organization. They are therefore difficult to reach. Local residents also need to be given a great deal of information about proposed tourism development so they can evaluate tourism among their other employment options and decide how they want to interact with tourists. This evaluation may take time, but it is essential to the process.

Aside from ethical or moral considerations, it is important to incorporate local communities into ecotourism planning because not doing so may prove disastrous for the tourism industry. If local populations do not participate actively in all aspects of developing and managing natural resources for tourism and benefit from this enterprise, they may choose to use the natural resources in other, perhaps less sustainable ways. These alternative land uses, such as logging, mining, slash-and-burn agriculture, or poaching may threaten the integrity of the resources, and thereby the ecotourism product.

The ecotourism business is in its infancy. Individuals, agencies, and organizations across the public and private sectors are analyzing, promoting, controlling, and investing in this industry. They must be encouraged to work together if ecotourism is to be beneficial for both conservation and economic development. Otherwise, the current wave of enthusiasm for ecotourism will die for lack of beautiful places to visit.

A comprehensive framework for planning ecotourism needs to be put in place to both maximize potential benefits and minimize the potential costs for people and the environment. Following is a description of the framework we developed based on the study.

FRAMEWORK FOR PLANNING, DEVELOPING, AND MANAGING ECOTOURISM

PREPLANNING

Before the planning process begins, representatives from various governmental ministries (planning, public works, finance, budget, tourism, agriculture, forestry, parks, environment, education) should meet to discuss how ecotourism fits into the nation's development goals. This judgment is based on a preliminary assessment of the country's ecotourism product, specifically the attractiveness and special features of its natural areas and carrying capacities, and the demand for ecotourism. Input should be solicited from park managers, the private sector, international funding agencies, local conservation groups, and native communities. If the government representatives agree that ecotourism ought to be included as a component of the national development plan, an Ecotourism Board should be created to further investigate the status and potential of nature tourism. The board should consist of members from government, park managers, tour operators, the private sector, local conservation organizations, and native communities. International development and conservation organizations may be invited to provide financial and technical assistance.

The role of the Ecotourism Board is to create a strategy for ecotourism growth. The board will oversee planning, development, and management functions.

ECOTOURISM PLANNING, DEVELOPMENT, AND MANAGEMENT STRATEGIES

Environmentally sound ecotourism growth must be seen as a long-term activity. While many natural areas already attract tourists and need to respond immediately with a short-term plan, it is essential that every natural area have a documented strategy of how tourism will be promoted and controlled over the long term.

In the following recommendations, native communities are recognized as a key component to success. However, given the difficulties of identifying each group, they are not singled out as a target group. The responsibility for including native communities in ecotourism growth is placed with local conservation organizations. These organizations are generally familiar with native groups in the areas where they work and can solicit representation or interaction as needed.

Many of the recommendations are repeated under several target groups. These groups need to work together on a particular task or step. Collaboration among all groups is critical at each stage.

PLANNING

At this stage in the process, the current and projected status of the country's natural resources and ecotourism industry is assessed. It is important to remember that most ecotourism so far has occurred spontaneously with little encouragement; however, with proper planning, the benefits of ecotourism can be maximized and the drawbacks minimized.

Recommendations for Ministries

Ministry of Tourism

- Allocate a portion of the budget for nature tourism development.
- Work with other ministries to develop an entrance fee system for parks and reserves. Use differential fee structures for foreigners and nationals when appropriate.
- Work with other ministries to design a financial mechanism to channel a portion of entrance fee revenue back into the maintenance and protection of the protected area.
- Change tourism laws and policies as needed to include environmental protection clauses for natural areas.

- Design visitor surveys to collect statistical information on current status of tourists.
- Develop visitor count mechanisms to record tourist data at park sites.

Ministry of Planning, Public Works

Evaluate nature tourism development within context of other development plans for the country.

Ministry of Agriculture, Forestry, Parks, Environment

These ministries are listed together because in most countries several are responsible for the management of natural areas.

- In the national protected area system plan, identify those wildland units where nature tourism will be developed and those where it will be discouraged.
- Create management plans for each protected area. Include tourism components for those areas with visitors (present or potential).
- In individual park budgets, take into consideration those parks that have tourists and need additional funds to cover personnel and tourist management training.
- Change protected area legislation as necessary to reflect ecotourism requirements.
- Work with park managers to create a data base of natural resources for each protected area.

Ministry of Budget, Finance

- Increase budgets of protected areas attracting tourists to enable these sites to control and provide for visitors.
- Participate in establishing the entrance fee collection scheme and rechanneling money back into parks.
- Design self-financing mechanisms for parks and reserves based on tourism revenues.
- Create tax and import exemptions to encourage private sector involvement in tourism development.

Recommendations for Park Managers

- Conduct full inventory of each protected area that receives tourists now or in the future. Inventory should include biological information about natural resources, statistics on current level of tourism, the present level of infrastructure development, the level of interaction between local residents and park facilities, the fragility of the ecosystem, and the ecological constraints to tourism development.
- Include nature tourism plans in operational, management, or master plans for individual protected areas. Ensure that nature tourism plans comply with park management objectives, guidelines, and zoning.
- Work with other ministries to develop mechanisms for entrance fees and for channeling money back to the parks.

Recommendations for Tour Operators and the Private Sector

- Evaluate the current and potential tourism market through surveys and other information sources.
- Design mechanisms for channeling a portion of nature tourism profits back into park maintenance.
- Participate in design of guidelines for "environmentally sound" tour operators and tourists.

Recommendations for Local Conservation Organizations

- Decide if tourism development and management is part of the organization's mission and how this fits with the other objectives of the organization.
- Solicit the participation of native communities surrounding natural areas to determine the extent to which they want to become involved with tourism development and management.
- Select local representatives to be included in every step of tourism planning.

- Solicit financial and technical assistance from international conservation and funding organizations for tourism development and management as necessary.

Recommendations for International Development and Conservation Organizations

- Develop a roster of international nature tourism consultants with expertise in various angles of tourism development and management, such as ecological architecture, community participation in tourism, wildland management and tourism, etc.
- Develop a set of guidelines for "environmentally sound" tour operators and tourists.

DEVELOPMENT

Recommendations for Ministries

Ministry of Tourism

- Work with private sector and international funding agencies to develop appropriate tourism infrastructure at each site. Keep in mind the importance of offering opportunities for tourists to spend money so that there is a benefit to the park and local people.
- Work with the park service and tour operators to create training programs for park personnel and tour guides. Training should include natural resource education and tourism management skills.

Ministry of Agriculture, Forestry, Parks, Environment

- Develop environmental impact studies and mechanisms to determine carrying capacity limits for each protected area.
- Hire adequate park personnel to maintain parks and to control tourists.
- Work with the Ministry of Education to develop environmental education materials for park sites and to create

information about ecotourism for schools.
- Set up mechanisms for entrance fee collections and for channeling the income back to parks.

Ministry of Budget, Finance

- Set up mechanisms for channeling income from tourism revenues into park maintenance.

Ministry of Education

- Create a training program for local guides that covers natural history, special features of the area and country, tourism management and languages.
- Develop environmental education materials for tourists and materials about ecotourism as it relates to natural resource conservation for local schools.
- Provide training for environmental education administrators who will distribute the above materials.

Recommendations for Park Managers

- Assist in development of park infrastructure to ensure it is environmentally sound. This may include a visitors' center, snack bar/restaurant, restrooms, gift shop, and other facilities that would enhance a tourist experience and generate funds. Use local labor and products when possible.
- Create effective trail system and interpretive programs for parks.
- Provide necessary training for park personnel.
- Give preference to local residents in hiring park personnel and offering concessions within the park.
- Collect baseline data on natural and cultural resources before and during promotion of tourism.
- Conduct environmental impact studies and establish "tolerable levels of visitation."
- Set up data collection system to gather visitor statistics.
- Select national and international tour companies that

will bring groups to the park.
- Develop guidelines for tourists to follow while in the park.

Recommendations for Tour Operators and the Private Sector

- Establish pretrip environmental education programs for tourists and work with park managers to develop on-site educational materials.
- Select and train local guides.
- Use local products in all nature tourism services.
- Work with tourism planners to create tourism packages that include a variety of natural resource attractions. These packages could be for groups or individuals. These may include nature-only tours or "add-on" nature extensions to other tours.
- Investigate the range of communication channels for publicizing ecotourism sites and activities.
- Some tour operators may choose to specialize in nature tours to enhance the diversity and quality of service they provide to nature tourists.
- Develop policy statements regarding "environmentally sound" tourism services.

Recommendations for Local Conservation Organizations

- Ensure that local communities remain actively involved with tourism development.
- Assist in coordinating activities between international funding agencies and park managers.

Recommendations for International Development and Conservation Organizations

- Facilitate public and private cooperation in developing tourism infrastructure as needed.
- Provide assistance for training programs for guides, park managers, environmental educators, and others.
- Fund and support technical assistance for parks, includ-

ing inventory studies, carrying capacity studies, zoning and land use plans, revision or elaboration of park management plans to integrate tourism needs, and tourism monitoring mechanisms.
- Fund and support studies of sociocultural impacts and considerations in nature tourism development.
- Fund and support case studies of tourism development at selected parks to use as models for other parks.

MANAGEMENT

Recommendations for Ministries

Ministry of Tourism

- Monitor the quality of nature tourism services and facilities.
- Create promotion and marketing schemes for parks that want more tourists or want to regulate tourist arrivals, eliminating crowded peak seasons and dull low seasons.

Ministry of Agriculture, Forestry, Parks, and Environment

- Continue to monitor the economic and environmental impacts of tourism and evaluate whether the costs of tourism are outweighing the benefits in any natural areas. Take appropriate steps to remedy this problem if it emerges.
- Evaluate whether the system of wildlands is adequate for the tourism demand or if more areas need to be created as tourism destinations.

Ministry of Budget, Finance

- Ensure that parks that have the most visitors are being compensated to cover additional costs of personnel and training.

Ministry of Education

- Continue to create educational programs about tourism and the environment. Conduct surveys of students and tourists to determine the impacts of these programs.

Recommendations for Park Managers

- Monitor tourism at sites to see that tourists comply with park guidelines.
- Conduct economic and environmental impact studies and publicize any essential information.
- Evaluate the effectiveness of interpretative materials and adjust them if necessary.
- Periodically survey tourists' characteristics, motives, and activities for use in developing future tourism policies and promotional plans.
- Monitor park personnel and guide training programs to make sure they are keeping up with tourism demand.

Recommendations for Tour Operators and the Private Sector

- Work with public sector to ensure that ecotourism services meet international standards.
- Offer continuing education for guides to diversify their expertise.
- Work with park managers to redistribute tourism during high season and in areas with high levels of visitation through marketing and promotion schemes.
- Continue to make a financial contribution to parks and encourage other tour operators to do so.

Recommendations for Local Conservation Organizations

- Ensure that native groups are involved with tourism to the extent they want and that they receive proper training for their work in tourism.
- Ensure that natives have access to adequate markets for their handicraft goods and other products.

Recommendations for International Development and Conservation Organizations

- Fund and support seminars on creative financing and policy forums for nature tourism.

- Fund and support case studies of tourism management at selected parks to use as models for other parks.

REFERENCE

Boo, E. 1990. *Ecotourism: The Potentials and Pitfalls.* Washington, D.C.: World Wildlife Fund-U.S.

CHAPTER 10

Global Solutions:
An Ecotourism Society

MEGAN EPLER WOOD

Tour operators and ecotourists have begun to make the conservation of natural areas a priority. A number of operators now feature tours on which clients clean up tourism sites that have suffered negative impacts from overuse by visitors. More and more tour operators are allocating a portion of their client fees to conservation groups at home or abroad. Some travel groups even have their own nonprofit foundations that fund conservation projects in destination countries.

For the most part, these steps have been taken without coordination. Working together, tour operators, conservation groups, local communities, and host governments could have a far greater impact on the conservation of natural areas. We therefore propose to found an Ecotourism Society, offering the opportunity for specialists in tourism and conservation to learn from each other and develop a global initiative for the conservation of ecotourism areas.

Developing the initial focus and agenda of the Ecotourism Society will be a challenge. The society must bring together specialists from many different fields—sociology, anthropology, biology, ecology, international studies, economics, development, and others. It must recruit and win the support of travel professionals and natural resource managers. Representatives from government and local communities must be included. Whether ecotourism is only a fad or a genuine conservation tool will depend, in large part, on the ability of these diverse constituencies to work together.

The first task is to reach agreement on what ecotourism is, and what it is not. Our definition embraces both environment and economics: ecotourism is purposeful travel to natural areas to understand the cultural and natural history of the environment, taking care not to alter the integrity of the ecosystem while producing economic opportunities that make the conservation of natural resources financially beneficial to local citizens.

The society's main focus will be to build ecotourism's potential as a tool for sustainable development. The market for environmental tourism has grown so rapidly that it has become an important source of foreign exchange in countries such as Ecuador, Kenya, and Costa Rica. The Ecotourism Society can formulate models and guidelines for governments, nongovernmental organizations (NGOs), and private entrepreneurs that will help them develop ecotourism projects that are both economically and environmentally sound.

There are many natural areas that desperately need the economic contribution that a well-managed ecotourism program can offer. The Ecotourism Society can provide technical assistance and promotion for the regions that most need ecotourism to help them conserve their natural areas. It will recommend site planning and management techniques to ensure that ecotourism development does not place undue stress on the environment and that the economic contribution makes its way to the host country and local communities. Ultimately, the Ecotourism Society will develop and promote model ecotourism programs that will identify new destinations, thereby alleviating the pressures on today's most popular destinations.

In addition, the society can play a leading role in devel-

oping regional ecotourism action plans that identify solutions for ecotourism sites suffering from stress caused by
overuse. Destinations in countries such as Kenya, Nepal,
and Peru are already having serious trouble with excess garbage, off-the-road driving, wildlife harassment, and water
pollution. And Antarctica, with no governing body in place
to oversee and limit visitation, is in serious jeopardy of losing its pristine character due to its increasing popularity as
an ecotourism destination.

While the Ecotourism Society will work toward developing "clean" ecotourism and appropriate ethics among travel
organizations, it will not endorse specific operators. This
would limit participation and ultimately hinder cooperation
within the travel community.

As a first step in developing and gaining support for the
Ecotourism Society, we circulated a list of objectives for
comment among travel operators and conservation organizations. The following is an annotated version of that document.

ECOTOURISM AND INTERNATIONAL DEVELOPMENT ASSISTANCE

The Ecotourism Society should help put ecotourism at the
top of the agenda of multilateral development and financial
institutions. Currently, large tourism developments with
large profit potential due to high volume receive the most
favorable treatment. Ecotourism will never generate as
much revenue as "mass tourism." Nevertheless, new criteria
need to be established that place a value on the preservation
of rain forests, watersheds, biological diversity, and other
economic intangibles. The Ecotourism Society should:

- Develop and implement alternate models of economic
  analysis that place a value on the conservation of natural resources, specifically as related to ecotourism developments.
- Propose management strategies that channel tourism

revenues into community development and environmental protection.

- Coordinate feasibility studies in specific countries with potential for ecotourism development.
- Build a database of economic and natural resource data for ecotourism developments in specific regions and countries worldwide.

RESEARCH AND PUBLICATIONS

Until very recently, no school in the United States devoted a full course of study to tourism and its impact on natural resources. Yet, a quickly expanding group of students and professionals are eager for further information on the management of visitors in parks and natural areas. Tour professionals have all expressed a strong interest in environmental guidelines. A number of organizations such as the National Audubon Society and the American Birding Association have adopted travel codes of ethics for their membership. The time is right to generate a series of professional papers on ecotourism that would be accessible to the general public, tour agencies, conservation organizations, and the academic community.

In addition, the society ought to:

- Publish a series of papers, entitled "Principles of Ecotourism," that would review issues of concern to ecotourism professionals, such as camping etiquette, waste disposal in remote areas, environmental impacts of jet skis, etc. These papers would be edited by the society.
- Encourage the study of visitor impacts in natural areas by graduate environmental studies programs, in management plans of protected areas, and in ongoing research programs in natural areas worldwide.
- Cooperate with the academic world, nongovernmental organizations, and tour operators to develop guidelines for carrying capacities in ecotourism sites.

LOCAL PARTICIPATION

The most important area for action is also the most daunt-
ing. If ecotourism is to make an important contribution to
sustainable development, projects must provide direct benefits to local peoples. Conservation International, the Man
and Biosphere Program, and World Wildlife Fund, among
others, have recommended the establishment of ecotourism
programs as a way to provide economic incentives for conservation. Yet, there is no network in place to implement
these recommendations. In most countries, tourism officials
do not have a grasp of resource conservation management
issues, nor do they interact with the professionals who do.
Local conservation organizations generally are not prepared
to establish ecotourism programs since they lack business
acumen and expertise in the travel arena.

The Ecotourism Society proposes to introduce informed
and interested individuals into a worldwide network, using
the "in-bound tour operator" as liaisons. In-bound tour companies run the ground operations for many of the foreign-
based ecotourism operators. They are highly knowledgeable
about nature tourism destinations in their countries. They
could be an effective core of support for the development of
sound ecotourism policies in each nation and could play an
important role with the society.

Other priorities of the Ecotourism Society include:

- Building grass roots networks of local tour operators, region by region.
- Forming regional committees, including tour operators,
  local nongovernmental officials involved in tourism policy, tourism officials, natural resource managers, and
  transportation specialists.
- Using this network to gather preliminary data on the regional economic and social framework needed for the
  successful development of ecotourism projects.
- Accessing preliminary data to create standardized research instruments that will help identify the elements

necessary to implement regional ecotourism programs (e.g., training, infrastructure, financial resources, information networks, and technical assistance). This information will help the society formulate a series of regional action plans recommending which projects to target for investment and support in each area.

ECOTOURISM CLEARINGHOUSE

As the society develops its agenda, a wide variety of interest groups will look to it for in-depth information: out-bound tour operators (nature tour packagers in the United States); in-bound operators (nature tour organizers in destination countries); nongovernmental organizations (environmental groups, universities, and associations involved in ecotourism tours, policies, and projects); park management professionals involved in tourism; international and domestic governmental officials concerned with setting policy related to tourism and conservation of natural resources; retail travel professionals; travel writers and communicators; tourists seeking information on ecotourism.

Almost everyone working in the field of ecotourism feels frustrated by the lack of centralized information available on ecotourism projects. The society clearly needs to develop databases and a reference service on people and institutions actively working on ecotourism projects; background information on existing programs, guidelines, and management plans; and cutting-edge information on how to plan for the economic and environmental impacts of ecotourism.

FINANCIAL SUPPORT

The society will look to membership contributions and grants for its initial financial base. It will consult with major financial institutions that need alternate methods to evaluate the economics of ecotourism development based on the value of sustained natural resources. Support will be sought from the foundation and corporate communities. In addition, the organization will market its "Principles of Ecotourism" series. The goal is to start small, build a strong project base, and develop institutional supporters. This agenda will ensure that the society becomes a recognized source of information and policy initiatives on ecotourism.

CONCLUSION

Many professionals are struggling to find the delicate balance that will make ecotourism a positive force for sustainable development. Even the most responsible tour operators have witnessed the nightmare of seeing destinations they carefully opened to tourism destroyed by other companies following in their tracks. Once destinations become popular, there is often no way to control visitation. Some environmentalists have suggested that moratoriums are needed for areas that have suffered from too much tourism. Such a ban could be implemented successfully only with the participation and planning assistance of the tourism community.

The Ecotourism Society will be the first organization to bring together the people, institutions, and information necessary to make informed recommendations on ecotourism policies. We will provide a forum for discussion and ideas. And we will provide critical information to tourism and business communities seeking to make their operations environmentally sound.

As the battle over the earth's remaining natural resources intensifies, the promise of tourism revenues will be a valuable bargaining chip for the conservation cause. The Ecotourism Society can help monitor and guide the development of this promising new source of revenue and support for conservation.

For more information write: Ecotourism Society
c/o Ecoventures LTD
P.O. Box 755
N. Bennington, VT 05257

ABOUT THE EDITOR

Tensie Whelan is vice president for Conservation Information at the National Audubon Society. She has worked as a journalist in Central America and is a former editor of *Ambio*, the international environmental journal produced under the auspices of the Royal Swedish Academy of Sciences. A graduate of the School of International Service at American University, Ms. Whelan holds a masters degree in International Communication. She is currently on the boards of the Rainforest Alliance and *E* Magazine.

ABOUT THE CONTRIBUTORS

Elizabeth Boo is assistant to the Director of the Latin American–Caribbean Program at the World Wildlife Fund-U.S.

Bill Bryan is president of Off-the-Beaten-Path travel agency in Montana.

John A. Dixon is an environmental economist at the World Bank.

Susan P. Drake is the United Nations Representative for the U.S. Environmental Protection Agency, Office of International Activities.

Dennis Glick is director of the Greater Yellowstone Tomorrow Project at the Greater Yellowstone Coalition.

Tom Grasse is Director of Marketing and Public Relations, International Expeditions, Inc.

Perez Olindo is Senior Associate at the African Wildlife Foundation in Kenya and was formerly director of the Kenya Wildlife Department.

Yanina Rovinski is a communications and ecotourism specialist at the Central American Office of the International Union for The Conservation of Nature and Natural Resources.

Richard Ryel is president of International Expeditions, Inc.

Paul Sherman is an economist for the Hawaiian state government.

Megan Epler Wood is president of Ecoventures, a communications consulting firm specializing in the environment.

INDEX

ALSO AVAILABLE FROM ISLAND PRESS

Ancient Forests of the Pacific Northwest
By Elliott A. Norse

*Balancing on the Brink of Extinction: The Endangered Species Act
and Lessons for the Future*
Edited by Kathryn A. Kohm

Better Trout Habitat: A Guide to Stream Restoration and Management
By Christopher J. Hunter

*Beyond 40 Percent: Record-setting Recycling
and Composting Programs*
The Institute for Local Self-Reliance

The Challenge of Global Warming
Edited by Dean Edwin Abrahamson

Coastal Alert: Ecosystems, Energy, and Offshore Oil Drilling
By Dwight Holing

The Complete Guide to Environmental Careers
The CEIP Fund

Economics of Protected Areas
By John A. Dixon and Paul B. Sherman

Environmental Agenda for the Future
Edited by Robert Cahn

*Environmental Disputes: Community Involvement in
Conflict Resolution*
By James E. Crowfoot and Julia M. Wondolleck

*Forests and Forestry in China: Changing Patterns of
Resource Development*
By S. D. Richardson

The Global Citizen
By Donella Meadows

Hazardous Waste from Small Quantity Generators
By Seymour I. Schwartz and Wendy B. Pratt